GRIMS' NEW FAIRY TALES

OF LOVE OVERCOMING EVIL

BRIAN & JULIA BETH GRIM

© 2021
ISBN: 978-1-7363461-0-5

Dedication

To our children, now with children of their own.

Melissa aka Malika aka Ge Tian-en (God's grace)

Joel Quedar aka Yusup aka Ge Tian-ci (God's gift)

Andrew 'Sarkus' aka Nurullah aka Ge Tian-fu (God's happiness)

Abigail aka Adalet aka Ge Tian-le (God's completion)

Contents

Introduction	i
Preface	1
Lights Out	1
The Coffee Bean	2
The Fortuneteller's Tea	3
Patti Lee	7
The Canisters	8
Whiskers	14
The Puppy Who Was a Boy	15
Hero of the Hill	20
The Cabinetmaker	22
When Things Get Deep	29
A Broken Needle	30
The Last Words of Sir Diggery	32
The Horse Herd	33
The Kitchen	43
Furniture Talk	44
A Highland Lament	50
Feather Quills	52
Good Queen Jill	59
The Ferryboat Puller	61
We'll die without pizza!	66
The First Fairy	67
Soup du Jour	74
The Pub by the Dock	76
Helios, Move Over!	82
Earth - Moon Talk	83
The Last Cent	87
The Street Sweeper	89
A Tiny Little Man	97
The Signmaker and His Son	98
Hyena's Love	104

The Candle on the Shelf 105
The Falling Tree 110
A Note in the Bottle 111
The Queen and Her Bee 119
Poisoned Water 120
Franklin P. Schmittie 127
The Bird Caller 129
on edge of woods 139
Shipwrecked 140
Corn Trees in Autumn 150
The Icemaker's Family 151
Paper Dragon 155
The Chinese Laundry 157
'Long the Way 160
The Samovar 162
Yeast or Baking Powder? 171
The Magic Chalk 172
Barefoot Sandy 178
The Runner's Folly 179
Tiger, Tiger 194
The Kangaroo's Secret 196
The Serpent and the Fowl 204
The Pretty Peace Bird 206
Ms. Tack is Back 213
The Bridge 215
Sassy Judy 220
The Lady 222
Leather Rose 232
Cause for Alarm 234
The Architect and the Artist 235
Afterword 265

INTRODUCTION

Decades before the latest set of challenges facing the world today, we lived and worked in the USSR, a place which officially ended as Boris Yeltsin and others gathered in our NGO's office building in Soviet Central Asia to sign it away. Before and after that, we lived and worked in western China, where the United Nations reports that up to a million Uygur people are presently detained in reeducation camps. Two of our children were born there in the 1980s. The final chapter of our children's overseas upbringing was on the Arabian Peninsula during 9/11.

To make sense of the diverse forms of good and evil we encountered, it was natural that we should do so in the same way as another set of Grimms did long ago — through Fairy Tales. Although we wrote the tales to read to our four children as they were growing up in these far-flung lands, the tales are meant for adults, just like the original Grimms' tales were. *As C.S. Lewis said, "Someday you will be old enough to start reading fairy tales again."*

Those who have experienced the dark side of life will find soul mates in the characters and solace in the oft ironic twists of humor that allow love to triumph. As with the original Grimms' tales, they are designed to be shared orally with others. But even if only with yourself (at first), start with the shorter ones marked with ♪, which are lyrical and begging to be read aloud.

Brian & Julia Beth Grim

Annapolis, Maryland

You can find us online at https://grimsfairytales.com/

Preface

"Truly, as is often said, the lessons of our childhood make a wonderful impression on our memories; for I am not sure that I could remember all that was said yesterday, but I should be much surprised if I forgot any of the things I heard long ago." — from a Dialogue of Plato

Lights Out

Evil wants us to forget childhood. Love is childlike.

For hours on end I can get hooked inside the pages of a book: my eyes get glued in fixed array as I can't tear myself away; my hands are bound to front and back by pirates who make sneak attack on ship I've stowed away upon — my legs get stiff, I cannot run 'cos pirates hold a musket gun up to my head, "I'm almost done," I say half dazed unto my Mum who says, "Lights out!" and stops my fun.

The Coffee Bean

Evil cannot tolerate freedom. Love sets us free.

I long for the days when I grew wild and free, the days when the humans just liked to drink tea! I'd ripen in sunshine, then fall to the ground: by dying and drying my life would rebound. From inside my shell I would send forth a sprout, and after some seasons I'd be free to tout a bush full of offspring all looking like me. Beans, coffee beans, yes, a real family tree!

But woe to me now as I'm looking around, trapped in glass grinder about to be ground and put in some basket and scalded to death with no chance to sprout or to leave a bequest! A beverage most humans don't think twice about, unless by poor planning they must do without … but please think of me who was once wild and free, and free me by switching and drinking just tea.

The Fortuneteller's Tea

Evil wants to control a gift. Love gives freely.

There once was a teapot with a special power to announce a blessing on whomever poured tea from its spout. The teapot, looking in all ways like an ordinary teapot, spoke with a voice when tea was poured from it and pronounced a good fortune upon the one whose hand held the handle. Following the fortune, however, came a warning that to ever use the teapot again would bring a binding curse.

For ages no one had been tempted to challenge the teapot's final warning. Legendary stories of those who had were enough to stay anyone's hand. One such story told of a king who had just been promised a doubled kingdom. He poured twice and was immediately paralyzed. Another legend recounted the woe of a woman who "forgot" and merely desired another cup of tea. She was turned to stone, but her heart and mind went on living.

But the stories of the good things it predicted far outweighed the dark legends. In the evenings around household hearths and in public houses, there were always marvelous accounts of what good had befallen the people who had poured from it.

The teapot predicted the most wonderful and welcome events. It somehow could tell what kind of hand held it and what was most needed in that life to give it a boost of good fortune. When an old woman, widowed and childless, poured tea from it, the voice said, "You will not live out your days alone." Then true to the prediction, the old woman was found by a kindhearted and distant relative who took care of her until her last breath. When a farmer, who was doubly troubled by his sick milk cow and beset by blight on his crops, poured from the teapot, the voice said, "Plant corn next year and you will be saved from ruin." Sure enough, the farmer planted corn instead of wheat, harvesting enough to sell at a huge profit, and was able to buy another cow.

Even children were permitted a chance to pour from the teapot. Some of them were no doubt saved from a miserable life by the blessing they heard. One boy heard, "You are restless in school because you are smart. Write stories and one day you will touch the heart of a nation." Only the boy himself knew how close he was to dropping out of school to join the circus.

The most often told story was of a poor mother of seven who boiled the water for the tea. Her seven children watched and waited with hopefulness that the blessing would fill their hungry bellies and warm their naked feet. With great reverence and ceremony, the mother poured out the tea into her cup which was chipped and missing its handle. The voice from teapot said, "Your husband has not — as all think — been executed for treason. He will be returning to you soon. Prepare to move into the castle." The woman's husband had been arrested as a spy and sentenced to death. However, it had all been a ruse to confuse the enemy, since in reality, he was a double agent in the service of the King. With the war won, the truth could be told and the husband was to be given a military command with highest honors — Captain of the King's Guard. No other story could top this one for irony.

And so, each person who poured from the teapot was blessed with gratifying news or a promise or some guidance. But as always, the blessing was followed up with a warning: "If again you pour from me, a curse you will receive."

Then one day it came to a woman who most certainly believed in blessings and curses, but who was skeptical that what came out of a teapot could be trusted, as she was a fortuneteller. She felt that her reputation for predicting the future was well established and she abhorred the idea that some pathetic piece of pottery could be her rival. Nevertheless, the teapot had come into her town and she received it from her neighbor. She even made her pot of tea, though she did not put much stock in the teapot's validity. Just before she poured it, she pulled the curtains shut so no one else could see her or hear what was said. The teapot said, "You will save yourself from ruin if you give up fortunetelling and, instead, make a living by selling your embroidery and lace. You are soon to be discovered as a fraud."

The fortunetelling woman was astounded to hear such a warning from the teapot, but she recognized the warning for the blessing that it was, and in that moment, became a believer in the teapot. She realized that it could predict the future in a way which she never could. Her jealousy for the little figure of clay was replaced by admiration. She, indeed, decided to open a shop like it had said, but instead of selling handicrafts which she made, she would sell the blessings of the teapot. For if she was soon to be discovered as a fraud, what better protection was there than to sit behind the teapot and benefit from its reputation and its wisdom.

So instead of passing on the teapot to the next person, she bade that person come to her. With her curtains still drawn and herself acting reverently, she prepared the pot of tea for the next person, and when it was time to pour, she had that person take the handle. The blessings were spoken by the teapot for the person who held the handle to pour, and when their face brightened with the news, the woman asked for payment out of respect for the teapot.

In this way, the woman saved herself from ruin by using the magic of the teapot. Everyone came to her door and paid for their chance to hear their blessing, even those who would never have visited her as a fortuneteller. The teapot performed its job just the same as if it were moving about from house to house, and person to person.

Not everyone approved of what the woman had done with the teapot. Many felt that she was doing wrong to make money from a magic teapot which she had received just like all of those before her. But the woman told them that the teapot itself had told her to keep it so that it wouldn't be broken by the constant changing of hands.

There was one clever man who had not received his blessing yet from the teapot. He decided to visit to the woman. When he came into her house, he said he wanted to pay in advance. It had never happened before, and this pleased the woman. But he needed some help. He asked her to pull the moneybag from his pocket because both of his arms were in plaster casts. She gladly took the moneybag. While she went about preparing the tea, the clever man complimented the woman for doing a fine job making the blessings available to everyone, and he assured her that she was respected for keeping the teapot safe from other hands which might break it. The woman glowed in the kindness and aptness of his words, and when the tea was steeped, he said, "Would you mind pouring it out for me since my arms are broken?" Without a thought, the woman poured his tea.

At that, the teapot spoke not to him but to her, saying, "You are cursed for being twice a fraud. You shall become deaf, mute, and crippled. The money you have made from my blessings will rot and you will be friendless." When the voice of the teapot stopped, the man pulled off his fake plaster casts, picked up the teapot and left the woman, satisfied that his money had been well spent.

The teapot was then returned to its service of being handed from person to person, and no one dared to keep it or sell its blessings like the woman had done. In fact, it is still being passed around to this day. Perhaps, it will be coming to your village next.

♪

Patti Lee

Evil afflicts warriors twice. Love is their strength.

Once upon a time in a village by the sea lived a spry and happy girl, little darlin' Patti Lee. In her garden she would play quite imaginary games: all her flowers sweetly sing, and her trees do dance with rain. She makes everyone so glad, makes them very very glad.

In the cottage window sits, watching her while she's at play, an old soldier who's returned from a war far far away. In his mind he's still at war fighting battles fought before. When he loses them again, sleep does save him with a snore. Patti Lee keeps at her play; a flat rock becomes tea tray.

'Cross the sea there still is war where the young are dying for causes that can save the world — causes well worth dying for. One young soldier's in the front thinking of his cottage yard where his daughter is at play, where rose petals are her cards. Being gone is very hard, O so very very hard.

This young soldier and his dad people say are really mad, fighting wars so far away while a good life could be had working in the village streets as a constable, a cop, keeping home fires glowing warm as sweet Patti spins a top. Patti Lee keeps at her play all the while her dad's away.

When he comes back safe and sound, tales of war he will not tell as he plays out in the yard helping Patti build a well. All the pain he suffered there in a moment flees away 'cos he sees in Patti's eyes the reward of all he's paid — Patti Lee can freely play, she can freely freely play.

☙

THE CANISTERS

Evil suspects sacrifice. Love sacrifices.

The seven years of exile were over. Speaking out against the government had exacted a heavy toll on Dmitri and Galina. Not only were they sent away to do hard labor, they now had to begin all over again and with poor health and no money. At least they had their village to return to where friends and their cottage waited for them.

They watched the familiar scenery come into view. A passing farmer had given them a ride on his hay wagon, not even realizing who they were or what they had suffered. He might have been interested to know had not their disheveled appearance made him suspicious. He flicked his reins and kept his senses alert.

When Dmitri had last been in this region, he was strong and robust. His face had been full as well as his hair. It was no wonder that this neighborly farmer failed to recognize the man beneath the sunken cheeks and thinning hair. The same was true of Galina. Before the exile she had been radiant with the knowledge that she was soon to become a mother, and her figure was rounded and rosy. On this, her return, she was waxen and frail. The child had died at birth and there hadn't been another.

Yet, both were thrilled to be returning. Wasn't this the very day they had dreamed of all the days of their exile? For seven years in their daily brief time to speak to each other, "We'll soon be home" were the last words they whispered as the guards forced them to part at the fence separating the men from the women. Their lives had been built upon convictions about fairness and justice and equality, and when they had been singled out from their village as troublemakers and dissidents, they were glad to stand up for their beliefs. No one could dissuade them from pointing out the injustices. They knew there was a better way. But it had earned them exile.

Before the mock trail, some friends from their village had secretly expressed their sorrow and even privately pledged their support, but they hoped Dmitri and Galina would understand that they themselves had to lay low to avoid the risk of also being sent off to do hard labor. Galina and Dmitri had large hearts that could accept another's lack of courage and still believe they were true friends. In light of this, they asked their friends to keep certain household treasures for them while they were gone. They said it would be a long time until they returned and so their belongings might as well be used by others.

To one friend had been given bedding and rugs which, at the moment of Dmitri's and Galina's arrest, the friend had sorely needed. A leak in his roof had destroyed his own. To another friend, whose old parents were coming to live with him and his wife, was given a table and four wooden chairs that Dmitri had made himself.

To yet another comrade they had given three favorite canisters. These canisters had sat on their kitchen shelf in previous times holding the makings of bread — yeast, flour, and salt. They were airtight with the lids on, but their larger value lay in their decorative appearance. Sitting side by side they formed a complete scene of pastoral repose worked in a mosaic of miniature tiles.

As Dmitri and Galina neared their home, their hearts were filled with emotion. Here was their little cottage in their own home village, and it was the fulfillment of a long-desired dream to be coming up to the door. Curtains in other cottages were gently pulled aside as Dmitri and Galina approached the front of their cottage. No one rushed out to meet them as they had imagined, but their large hearts, which were undiminished by their years of hard labor, also forgave this display of timidness. They knew that first moments were always awkward even among good friends and they were prepared to wait for their welcoming, though in their oft-repeated dream it had been otherwise.

Their little cottage was barer than they had remembered, but it was their own private home where they could be together. The curtains still covered the windows, but all other furnishings were gone. It appeared that the rest of the village had also borrowed from them in their absence. The little plot of ground in the back was just as they had left it so many summers ago. The tomato stalks had withered and then frozen, as had the weeds that had grown up around them.

The first hesitant knock came. Dmitri and Galina exchanged hopeful looks of being received back into their village. It was an old lady at the door. Her terse words explained the bareness of their cottage and the reticence of their neighbors, "We didn't think you'd ever come back so we helped ourselves. Here are the things I borrowed." With that, she left a wheelbarrow of odds and ends, all showing much use and not very much care.

The friend who had borrowed the bedding and the rugs rapped confidently at the door. He welcomed them back as if they had been only on a vacation. Between chuckles and with loud words he recognized that they would be needing blankets, but since the ones they had loaned him were still in use upon his beds and he was quite attached to them now, he returned in their place the ones that had been damaged by water so long ago. They were now dried stiff and carried a bad smell and not a few holes. But he offered that these would serve royally after what they had just come from. "My wife is all in a stir," he added, "afraid that you'll want your rug back, and she doesn't know how our little Junior will be able to play if he doesn't have the rug to crawl on.

I told her not to worry, that you don't have a child, so you won't be needing your rug." With that he left and promised to come again after they were settled in.

The friend who had been loaned the four chairs and table trundled up to the door with a cart, but on the cart were stools and a low table. Without a word, he unloaded the shabby pieces and set them up as if they were fine furniture.

"I would like to return your own pieces, but my old parents have grown quite attached to them and besides, they are too old to sit on stools which have no backs. And as you are only two, you can eat on a small table. We are four and need more space." The man wished them a happy homecoming and left.

They saw no other neighbors that day, although every now and then something would be left outside their door that had been borrowed during their period of exile. Slowly their house began to be filled with the material goods of a home, all of it having once been theirs or a substitution for what had been theirs. Most noticeably, however, Dmitri and Galina missed the sounds and feelings of being welcomed home. The poor condition of the returned belongings only accentuated the poor quality of the village's acceptance of them.

It wasn't until the second day that the friend and neighbor who had borrowed the three canisters came by their cottage. Both Dmitri and Galina were working in the garden and didn't hear his knocking until it became pounding. He carried a bag into their cottage and set it down casually onto the low table. Without any reference to the contents of the bag, he plied them with questions about their exile, and begged them to forgive the aloofness of the other neighbors. "Everyone thought you were strangers when you came into town. Lucky for you that I recognized you. Some of the folks were going to come at you with pitchforks. Your appearance is a bit of a shock, but the villagers will come around to believe it's really you." Pledging his unwavering friendship and promising to stand up for them until the rest of the village could accept them, he left.

Dmitri and Galina were sobered to realize their appearance raised suspicion among the villagers. It truly felt like their exile was not over. At least they had the presence of each other which, except for one short conversation each day, they had not had during their seven years away.

They both turned toward the bag on the table expecting to find their treasured canisters that would redeem the drab appearance their cottage now had. Opening the bag, Dmitri put in his hand and lifted out a common pottery vessel with a piece of warped wood for a lid. He reached for the next one, hoping that only one of the beautiful canisters had been replaced. The second container was like the first, only with a large chip missing at the lip. Still with anticipation that the third might be one of the works of art, he pulled out another common brown pottery container, and this one with a crack running down the side. It couldn't be denied that the three canisters before them, cracked and chipped and only one with a lid, a warped lid, reflected their own alteration from being healthy, vibrant, respectable people, to being sallow, sober, and shunned. The more their things were returned to them, the more they understood their pathetic position.

They summoned their courage to rebuild their life and their place in the village. It appeared more difficult now than when they had done it before. All their resolve was required to not become embittered, especially as they had survived the exile without being broken. However, their former jobs would not be given back to them and they were faced with the need to survive, yet without the means to do it.

One bleak evening when the fullness of being ostracized settled heavily upon them, they sat staring at the empty broken canisters. Of all their unreturned possessions, they mourned the loss of the three beautiful canisters the most, for they felt their beauty would have given them hope that they too could become beautiful again. But at the moment, nothing but tears would fall over the empty broken canisters, and the tears turned to deep sobs as the full weight of being broken themselves was realized.

When their grieving had abated with the flow of tears, they stared in wonder at the three canisters. Assuming they were seeing something that wasn't there, they blinked and rubbed at their eyes. Finally, they touched with their fingers and verified the presence of yeast in one canister, flour in the second canister, and in the third, a spice which appeared to be sugar or salt, but was different from either. How they came to be filled was unexplainable, a mystery.

Mystery or not, Dmitri and Galina decided to make a loaf of bread to console their hearts and assuage their hunger. When it was made, they ate it in awe. No bread had ever tasted so light and airy, and the spice seemed to build a fire in their veins. Even the smell of it baking had been unusual. While they ate it, they became aware of people passing to and fro outside their kitchen window.

A neighbor with the most pluck knocked on the door with some lame excuse, and then asked what made that unusual smell. With no shame, he even asked to taste a piece of bread, and further, if he could take a bit home to his wife. Dmitri and Galina discovered that their hearts were still large and that they could forgive the wavering of friends and neighbors. To anyone who came that evening they gave a taste of bread until the whole loaf was gone.

The next day, however, much to their surprise, the canisters were not as they had left them the night before. They were full to the brim of yeast, flour, and spice. So, much as people who are making their way out of a dark tunnel following only the pin prick of light, Galina and Dmitri began to make bread. The aroma wafting on the breeze was the only advertisement needed. Before the first loaf was out of the oven, a group was gathered outside of the door. When they began to ask if they could have a taste, Dmitri answered, "Of course. We sell it by the loaf. Who's buying today?"

From that day onward, the canisters never went empty and Dmitri and Galina were known for their large hearts and their bread.

♪

WHISKERS

Evil cannot comprehend poetry. Love is poetry.

I have decided that to write in standard poetry does seem quite trite and is a form of genteel snobbery. So, I'll try to break this habit and just think in plainer prose; but 'tis rather like a rabbit who must stop his twitching nose.

Still, here I go! Yes, I shall try to make that poet stop! But science says the hare will die if he must crawl, not hop.

Well, never mind; a poet's mind can think in more than verse. It's just that words that fail to rhyme have whiskers far too terse! They scratch and stiffly addle hope in bunny-brains like me. But whiskers of a poet's hand grow soft and long and free! I love these words with fluffy fur, 'cos twixt these floppy ears I know the human side of life does prick too many tears.

Alas, I see that I must write in standard poetry, 'cos bushy tails and fuzzy paws redress humanity.

☙

THE PUPPY WHO WAS A BOY

Evil cannot empathize. Love enters the other's world.

When Toby went to sleep the night before his tremendous adventure, he was a cocker spaniel puppy. As he always did, he slept beside Tommy, his boy. Both were excited. Tommy was going to First Grade the next day and was too wound up to sleep. But when Tommy did fall asleep, he kicked his legs and thrashed around. Somehow, in all the kicking and thrashing of Tommy, a strange thing happened to Toby.

The first sign that something unusual had happened was when a shirt was being pulled over Toby's head. He wiggled this way and that to get out of the dark tunnel, and finally he did come out into the light again, but only to feel the buttons being fastened and his arms being bent and twisted into the sleeves. Toby-the-puppy thought that he was dreaming because nothing like this had ever happened before in all of his twelve weeks.

While contemplating the strangeness of this dream, Toby was buckled up around his middle and, looking down, saw a pair of long trousers on his legs. Without any time to consider how he was to play with these legs braces on, his paws were thrust into shoes and tied snugly to keep them from falling off, but Toby thought the best thing for them to do was to fall off.

Tommy-the-boy was now in the body of the cocker spaniel, and Toby-the-puppy was in the body of the boy. Just as Toby-the-puppy realized that he was really the one being dressed, he saw Tommy-the-boy lift a lazy eyelid from the protection of the bed covers. There was something in that lifted eyelid. Toby-the-puppy adored his boy Tommy, but he had never wished that he could become a boy. So perhaps it was Tommy's wish to become a puppy that had caused this mysterious exchange of bodies.

Whatever had happened, Toby-the-puppy looked like a boy — and all boys were sat down at the breakfast table and told to eat quickly and quit dawdling since the bus is coming and there is still a lot to do, such as brush your teeth and comb your hair and pick up your school bag and don't forget your lunch money and, oh yes, behave yourself at school today. Toby was mounting the school bus steps when he looked back wistfully at his house, and there was Tommy-the-boy in a puppy body looking out the window at him. Toby waved, but he was not very happy to be climbing into a strange yellow machine while his puppy body was safe at home.

Toby followed the crowd as best he could, which meant he followed a lot of school bags. Before he knew it, he had followed them inside some big doors and the big doors had closed behind him, and there he was, a little puppy in a big strange building, squashed in the middle of a big crowd of children. If he had known how big and scary the school would look, he wouldn't have followed the other children in. He would have made his getaway when he got off the bus, like any good puppy would have. He was just eyeing up the big doors to see if there was a crack in them so he could make a break for it when a very tall lady with very tall hair and very wide glasses laid her very long hand across his shoulder. She said a lot of things in long drawn-out words, and Toby heard her say the name of his boy Tommy, and he felt himself propelled along next to the lady's very long legs and he noticed her very long feet, and then he was placed on a chair.

The tall lady went away to the end of the room and stood in front of a big desk. Toby thought she was the biggest lady he had ever seen, but Toby, being only a twelve-week-old cocker spaniel, hadn't really seen all that many ladies.

Toby saw that all the chairs were filled with children that looked about the same as Tommy, and with a sudden urge to find his boy, he frantically looked around. Then he realized that he was Tommy and, looking down, he did see Tommy's hands and feet and shirt, but what he couldn't see was Tommy's face. Just when he was trying to lick Tommy's cheek with his tongue, the tall teacher called out Tommy's name, and Toby-the-puppy looked up. He was supposed to raise up his arm and say "Here." He obeyed the tall teacher but his "Here" came out as a hushed whimper. The tall lady stopped and said, "You're not a baby anymore. You're in the First Grade now. Let me hear a big boy 'Here'." So, even though Toby wanted to say, "I am just a puppy," he let out a great big "Here," which made all the other children turn around to stare. The tall teacher said, "You needn't bark it out, just say it like a big boy."

Toby sat for as long as he could in his chair, and then his eye wandered to the window. There he saw the breeze blowing the leaves of a tree and he could smell the outdoor smell and he saw a big place to run and some things to go sniff, and all at once, he was standing at the window looking for a way to get out. A long hand was laid on his shoulder and the tall lady said, "Big boys must sit in their chairs until they are given permission to get up. You must never get up unless you raise your hand first."

So, Toby sat down and raised his hand. The tall teacher asked what he wanted. He said he wanted to go outside, and the tall teacher said, "No." Toby slunk down into his seat and some of the other children looked at him and laughed. He was so frustrated. He needed something to chew on. If he had been warned about going to school, he would have brought his rubber bone; but now he only had a pencil, so he put it between his teeth and began to chew away. The tall lady appeared and took away his pencil. She said some very long words way up there under her very tall hairdo, but Toby only heard, "Big boys don't chew their pencils."

With a hopeful thought that maybe there were other puppies who got mixed up with the bodies of their masters last night, Toby looked around the room. He noticed that some of the boys were sitting very still but some others were wiggling all over like he was. Watching more closely, he saw that some of them had even chewed the ends of their pencils. He decided to keep a watch on those fellows so that if the chance came, they might make a break for it.

All at once a sharp bell shocked his ears and some of those boys popped out of their seats and took off at a run. Toby was right behind them. He was sure they must be puppies to run like that. Outside in the place where he had spied the tree and the good places to sniff, the other boys were climbing about and some were throwing a ball. When the ball flew to one side, Toby chased it intending to bring it back in his mouth, but then he realized he had on Tommy's body, so he scooped it up in his hands. Suddenly, he was in the game. It was a glorious time! In an instant, his opinion of school was changed.

He laughed at himself for thinking that sitting in a chair was school. Playing in this big yard was school, and he was so glad that Tommy had changed bodies with him. But then, another sharp bell shocked his ears. To his utter dismay, all the children began to go inside. He tried to beckon them to stay out and keep doing school with him, but they were all in lines walking one behind the other. He stood staring at this strange behavior. There was one other boy standing beside him with his mouth open in awe, too. When they saw each other, they turned to head for the corners of the yard. Two long hands attached to two long arms descending from a very tall body took both of them by the shoulders and put them into the line of children.

Back in his seat feeling like a trussed-up turkey, the shoes came off of Toby's feet. The toes just pushed them off, and boy, oh boy, did it feel good. The air could circulate between the toes again. Toby was called to go up to the board and write with a fat piece of chalk, and when the tall lady looked down from her heights and saw Toby's toes, she let out a very long squeal. He was ordered to retrieve his shoes and cover up his toes and never do that again. The whole time he was stuffing and tying, the tall teacher kept saying some tall words, and long as well, the gist of which meant that shoes must be worn by big boys.

At the end of the day, Toby sat on the bus slumped in a seat feeling like big boy tears were about to fall from his eyes. He hadn't really known which bus to get on, and now he was looking at strange sights. He was sure he would never see his house again. Most of the children had all gotten off. Then all at once, Toby spied his house. In a flash he was up from his seat and out the door, running up his walk and springing into his living room.

Tommy, in the cocker spaniel body, jumped up onto Toby's knees and asked how it was being in First Grade. Toby thought at first of the tall teacher with the tall hair. But instead, he told Tommy all about playing in the yard with the ball and all the places to sniff and all the other boys who were really puppies inside. So, the next day when Tommy got onto the bus, he was bravely back in his boy body. As he mounted the school bus steps, he turned and waved at Toby whose paws were pressed against the bedroom window watching his boy Tommy get into the big yellow machine.

♪

Hero of the Hill

Evil judges the just. The just are loving.

The castle crumbled to the ground and Johnny plainly knew that all the eyes of heaven watched to see what he would do.

To run away and hide himself he knew would kill his soul; so, drawing sword, he stood atop a nearby grassy knoll. He hollered for all Brave to form a line behind his back, but to him rallied not a one to counter the attack which felled the walls of castle strong (the siege was just too great). Most Brave had fallen with the walls while Faint Hearts ran away.

Resolving that the last free hill he'd with his life defend, he dared the conquering enemy to send their bravest men . . . but send them only one-by-one. The enemy just laughed. Still, sport they saw in Johnny's cry, so one strode up the path.

But quick the sword of Johnny struck its mark with native skill, which made the foes below to yell, "Hey, let's play king-of-the-hill!" Around the hill stood thousand men who loved the sport of blood, and each one thrilled to think that he would siphon Johnny's blood.

The second man to mount the hill was mighty Master Khan. He'd killed a hundred men before — he looked for hundred-one. When Johnny's arm was sliced it bled and made the Master grin, but with his blade bold Johnny did with fury thus begin to show the Master that a soul, though wounded, can defend a free land with his very life: his weapon flew like wind.

The scoffers' thirst for blood did surge to see their Khan get hacked! They all began to charge the hill, but loud cry held them back: his voice was piercing, strong and sure, his words did stop their tracks. He cried, "The Ghost of Khan shall rise and fend off your attack unless you come just one-by-one until this day is done and darkness shrouds this barren hill; so, fight me one-by-one!"

With jeers and sneers they ground their teeth each time new head would roll; as red sun set, still, Johnny stood erect on sanguine knoll. When night did cover fallen foes, their comrades raised a cry and charged at Johnny in pitch dark to make that blaggard die!

… In morning light he walked alone where once the castle stood; the horde of foes had killed themselves to quench their thirst for blood.

The battle fought, he slipped away as Faint Hearts reappeared. They said he could have been their King except for one small fear: "We fear that with such bloody hands, with sword that's lost its shine, the values of our peaceful land — like love — will see decline."

Thus, true heroes and true heroines by nature fade away, since in their selfless gallantry they cannot force their way.

Adieu.

The Cabinetmaker

Evil corrupts callings. Love confirms callings.

A very long time ago when cabinetmaking was still in its infancy, there lived a young cabinetmaker. He made a very successful living building cabinets of all designs and for all purposes out of various woods. Where he had come by his great skill no one could tell, not even himself. When he sat down to work with wood, he became one with it. It was as if the wood was wild and raw but became tame and cultured under his tools. His father and his grandfather had been shoemakers, but he discovered his penchant for woodworking early in life, and no one ever suggested that he should be shaping leather and working with a needle instead of sanding wood and using a chisel.

Not all the cabinetmakers of that time used a styling chisel, but this cabinetmaker took especial joy in making a finely fitted cabinet which had artistic finishing touches. For this reason his cabinetry was much in demand. When a piece was delivered to a certain household and payment was made, the new owner felt that surely this was as sound a chest or wardrobe as could be made, but the flourishes upon the corners and around the edges made it worth more than the price paid.

As sometimes happens, this was one case where the skill and innate talent of the artisan was embraced and applauded by others of his profession. Though young, he would sit before a piece of wood and shape it into art as if he had years of experience to draw upon. The other cabinetmakers of his guild were in such awe of his natural talent that when they could imitate his techniques and be recognized for their efforts, they glowed with the thrill of success. The cabinetmaker was not averse to sharing his techniques with others, but in truth, none could imitate the infusion of art that went naturally into his craft.

The other cabinetmakers chose him as the president of their guild and with him as their leader and representative, they all felt their lowly trade had been raised. The making of common cabinets for home use was quickly becoming a noble and dignified profession.

It would have been best if the cabinetmaker had never heard what happened to the cabinets he designed and built and decorated. On the one hand, he would have been pleased to hear how a busy mother was so often relieved to have a chest with rounded edges instead of sharp, as her small boy of two years had a propensity for knocking his head against the furniture. If he had been able to see the admiring looks his cabinetry received as they were put into daily use, it might have offset the horror of the things that he actually heard.

He was in his shop the day a fellow cabinetmaker came in with the news. "Did you hear what happened up at the Manor House? Aye, it's a bit of tragic news. The governess locked the poor daughter up into the cabinet until she learned to obey, and the poor darling suffocated before the governess knew what was happening. Ah, the crime of it. What will her parents do when they return? The governess is a niece, I think. By the way, it was one of your cabinets she was locked up in."

That news hit the cabinetmaker like an awl to the heart. In that instance as his soul was revolting against the cruelty done to the young one, he wished he had not made his seams and joints so tight; perhaps he could have let a door hang askance.

There was surely wickedness aplenty in those days. There was no loss of means that people found to mistreat others. But it was beyond the cabinetmaker's imagination how one of his cabinets could be used in the machinations of the wicked. He involuntarily felt a sense of guilt that what his hands had created had been the cage for a child. He tried to go back to his work, but his hands folded up upon themselves. His usual senses were marred, and the thought of his misused cabinetry sunk him lower into despair.

Then another fellow cabinetmaker came into his shop as he sat hunched over his failed attempt at work. One look told the fellow that the cabinetmaker was discouraged, but he plunged ahead anyway.

"Oh, the tragedies we have in our town," he began. "I just heard the news from my wife who heard if from her sister who got it from her nephew who's a messenger boy, so it's pretty dependable, that the vicar locked up his wife in a chest for the better part of two days while he went away. It seems he suspected her of infidelity and wanted to give no chance that she made a tryst. The poor wife banged and pushed on the lid until she was hoarse and her knuckles were bleeding. It was only luck that brought the wife's brother to town on an unexpected visit. He let her out but had to break the lid with an ax. Can you believe the things you hear? Especially about the vicar. Who can you trust if not him? By the way, didn't you craft that chest for their wedding?"

The cabinetmaker hated himself for making the lock fit so snugly into the chest. He had admired the well-fitting mechanism when he made it, but to imagine that it was used for a prison for a wife made his soul shudder with grief and shame.

Close on the heels of that fellow came another artisan with the news that the chemist had poisoned his old mother. Naturally, his poisons were stored in the hutch that he had requested the cabinetmaker build for him. Everyone who went to the scene of the crime to look on the distorted features of the old woman also saw the solidly built and ornately decorated set of shelves.

At this, the cabinetmaker laid down his tools and took off his apron. He pulled down his shades and locked the door as he left his workshop. The orders he was leaving undone were not so much on his mind as the horrors that took place using his handiwork.

His father tried to console him. "Now we shoemakers know from the start that people are going to be walking in fair weather as well as foul. They may walk in goodness or wickedness, but all we do is sell them the shoes. Our pay is our last claim to where those shoes go and what they do. I advise you to think the same about your cabinets."

There was certainly the sound of rationality there, and common sense said the shoemaker was as right as rain, but still the cabinetmaker could not imagine sitting before his wood separated from his feelings. Into each piece he had put his sense that beauty belongs in the commonplace things of life.

The guild met without him at their next meeting, but his absence unsettled the feeling that they were an important and noble profession. A representative was sent to the cabinetmaker to make him see sense.

"Look," he said, "you're a sensitive sort and you mustn't take it so hard that people have done ill with your handiwork. You mustn't let it get to you and interfere with your work. Did you see the customers outside your shop looking for their pieces? You'll damage the name and reputation of all the others of us if you don't get back to your bench. Besides, you're our president. With winter upon us, we're facing a tough time with the wood suppliers and we can't have you shirking your duties to mourn the misuse of what you should have made with less attachment."

With that, he left the cabinetmaker, assuming he had set everything to rights. However, the cabinetmaker didn't pick up his tools or tie on his apron or lift up his shades. He couldn't look at a piece of wood without imagining in what vile way it would be used. For many weeks he was in this frame of mind and was on the brink of ruin, leaving everything undone, not collecting the money people owed him already, and not accepting any new orders. Those who had asked for his workmanship canceled their orders and took them elsewhere.

His fellow artisans replaced him as president and scoffed at his natural ability which hung like a curse over him now, saying, "What good is ability if it gets sacrificed to an overly sensitive conscience?" One more fellow cabinetmaker visited him at dusk on the day before his shop was to be repossessed by the landlord.

"I feel for you. I can see your point. But you can't let yourself go on without work. You're too old to return to your father's roof or to learn a new trade. Now I have an idea of how you can put your skill to use without mixing up your heart in it. We never, those of us down at the guild, never really knew how much heart you put into your work until all this happened. We tried to imitate your techniques and we got a lot of praise for trying, but you were still way out ahead of us. It has sort of come as a shock to realize that you can't really make your masterpieces anymore with your heart all twisted out of shape. Now please hear my suggestion with the good intent with which I say it. It's a job that you would know how to do and the work would be steady, and there's no doubt how the things will be used ... You could make coffins." A deep silence followed.

When the fellow cabinetmaker who had come with all good intent received no response, he left feeling he had done his duty and then some. He scorned the silence of the cabinetmaker whose shop would be repossessed tomorrow.

In the darkness of the night the cabinetmaker pondered on the words of all, helpful or harmful, and he remembered his own love of the wood and how it felt when it took shape beneath his hands and how it was like parting with a friend when he delivered a piece of furniture. He wondered how he could ever again enjoy the wood and marvel at the tight seams and joints and take pleasure in a well-constructed lock mechanism.

As he sat thus in thought, he lit a candle. As he did, the lyrics of a childhood lullaby his mother used to sing came to mind and silently coursed to his heart.

> The candle lit in winter deep
> does from my mind darkness sweep,
> chasing sullenness away
> with the dance of subtle ray;
> casting shadows without fear,
> in the glow warmth appears,
> turning night to coziness,
> it fills my room with peacefulness.

The flicker of the candle fell upon the wood at his feet and it almost seemed to move. Taking up his tools and laying the wood across his knees, he began to cut and to shape. So he sat through the night — alone, contemplative and active.

As the sun cast its first rays down the village streets, he looked at what he had wrought, and he smiled. It smiled back at him and he was glad. For this was nothing with a hinge or a seam or a lock or a joint. This was the figure of a smiling child, standing in innocence holding a flower. He set it aside where he could gaze at it and where it could gaze at him.

He picked up another piece of wood and began to cut and to shape. Out of his efforts emerged another figure. The cabinetmaker was comforted as he brought out first the hands and then the face. At just the moment the eyes were being brought to life, the landlord stepped into the shop to repossess it and evict the delinquent cabinetmaker. But he halted in his errand, and reverently picked up the figure of the smiling child holding a flower.

"Why, if it don't look the image of my darling granddaughter before the sickness took her." The landlord became lost in reminiscence and sat down silently in a chair. The cabinetmaker worked on oblivious to his visitor. Only silence and the soft sound of wood shavings falling to the ground could be heard. Dabbing at his eyes, the landlord asked, "Do you think you could part with this? My missus would sure be comforted if she could have this darling to look at. If you agree, I'll consider your rent paid in full for the next year."

Without any further words the landlord walked out with a treasure, and the cabinetmaker, though he knew wickedness would never cease, continued to craft beauty in the commonplace.

♪

When Things Get Deep

Evil dismisses experience. Love embraces it.

One day I crawled inside the shell of a turtle by the sea. The turtle made a place for me and promptly served up tea. I asked the turtle where he'd been before he hit the beach.

"I've been below the Surface World to a place that's out of reach for those who need to be on top, who run when things get deep."

I thanked the turtle for the tea and from his shell did leap!

A Broken Needle

Evil discounts suffering. Love feels the pain.

A lone woman sat in the doorway of her small house crying into her apron. Her frail body shook with each fresh sob, and her hair hung disheveled over her shoulders. Her dress was stained with wear, especially around her knees.

A chipper woman in a bright clean blue dress with flowers in her hair and a starched white apron tied around her abundant waist came merrily into view.

"Hello, Sister, and whatever is the matter on such a fine May day?"

"Oh, Esther, my needle has broken and I haven't another."

"Sister, what nonsense you talk. Who should be sewing or thinking of sewing on a day as glorious as this? Look about you and just cast your busywork to the breeze. Let singing with the birds be your work today."

"But, Esther, this little white dress has a tear in it and I must mend it."

"It is no cause for worry that it has a rend. Put on the kettle and let's have a cup of tea together."

"If only I could, Esther, but the bottom of my water kettle burned out while it sat upon the fire, so I cannot heat water."

"Sister, I'm not particular. Heat the water in your cooking pot. Don't let your small troubles destroy the splendor of a May morning."

"I cannot do that, either, Esther. All the firewood is gone. The last pieces of it burned up when I could not tend to it."

"Then forget the tea and just produce a slice of cake from your pantry. We can at least commune and pass some gossip."

"Alas, I cannot even produce a crust of bread, for while I wasn't looking, mice got into the pantry and spoiled all the food."

"Never mind, Sister. Fresh air and cool water are food enough on such a day as today. You must learn to be thankful for what you've got. At least I could get a hug from your darling daughter before I go on my way."

"Oh, don't you see, Esther? While the firewood went untended and the bottom of my kettle burned out and the mice were feasting in my pantry, my darling daughter lay dying in her crib. I must mend this dress to bury her in, and my needle is broken."

♪

The Last Words of Sir Diggery

Evil cares not about truth. Love seeks it and is truth.

    The water soaked his leather case and blurred the ink and thus erased from mortal time and memory the last words of Sir Diggery.

    He'd lived a life of Quest and Grace — a model for the human race; he'd found the key to happiness and wrote it down in humbleness. But on the road he was ambushed and left to die beside thorn bush. Then as the rain came beating down, some passerby who thus him found picked up the case and shrugged and said, "This is not yours since now you're dead."

    She dumped the refuse from within and thought she'd found a real bargain. She wiped her feet upon the mass of papers which contained the last ... the last words of Sir Diggery, thus cleanly wiped from memory.

The Horse Herd

Evil can't always predict goodness. Love expects it.

A young woman dressed in riding gear sat astride a chestnut Arabian. The horse and the young woman were well matched — both had excellent looks, immaculate form, and superior ability. The young woman should have been grieving, and in fact, feigned grief as she saddled her horse, declaring that she was so sad that only a ride upon the horse would keep her from going hysterical.

No one stood in her way. All the stable hands and household personnel had experienced her hysterical fits at least once in their tenure at this horse farm. When they had received blame for bringing it on, each privately thought that her father was too blind to the character flaws of his daughter. Nevertheless, they learned to stay clear and give way when she threatened hysterics. She rode her Chestnut as if all was well in the world, though her father was at that moment on his deathbed.

"Let him hurry up and get it over with" was the only thought in her heart. All this waiting and pretending to grieve was a trial for her. She had nothing to say to him in his last moments. She didn't need to hear one more time that he loved her. Once a day the sick room was graced by her presence, and during that hour, she went through the motions of a dutiful daughter while remaining aloof to his ailing form.

There was a will. He had mentioned it often. She was named as main beneficiary, though small bits of money were to be divvied up among the loyal staff. For years she had developed ideas for what she would do when she was in charge of the farm and had the money to back up her words. To fire some of the present staff and hire others was her first plan — others who could never compare her to her father.

She had been given the best equestrian training. Her father had hired a full-time trainer who made sure she won trophy after trophy when she competed. Lately, she had given up competing, first, to get rid of the trainer who had become too bossy, and second, to signal that she was beyond collecting a trove of cups and statues. She was ready to compete for things in the real world.

Being the prima donna of the riding ring had given her an additional edge over the stable hands. She could shame the oldest and trustiest of them just by pointing out something they had left undone and accuse them of trying to hinder her success. Her eye was sharp, as was her tongue, and most of the hired hands tried to melt into the shadows when she blew into the stable to saddle her horse.

To balance her selfish and acerbic nature, she had a true respect for the horse as a beautiful, awe-inspiring beast. To see them grazing in the field brought her soul its only repose. When she groomed a horse and felt its flanks ripple under the currycomb, she lost herself in wonder at its strength and yet its meekness. It was only in the quietness of grooming that she put aside her scheming tyrannical nature and experienced any quietness in her heart.

On this day, when she should have been grieving and keeping watch at the bedside, she worked her horse and herself, determined that her father's death would not cause her one moment of weakness, and that immediately, she would take charge and begin to issue the orders. At her same age, her father had been wild and independent, and it irked her that she was still managed. Only the promise by him that she would inherit the farm and the herd had kept her from giving free rein to her own wild and independent side.

While she jumped hurdles in the ring, she saw the housekeeper wave her arms above her head on the porch. "Bother," she thought, "the old man probably hiccupped and they are all in a panic." But, dutifully, she ended her riding and prepared once again to be the concerned and grieving daughter.

"Missy, you must come quick. Your father is calling for you. He has one last thing he must say."

"Probably," she thought, "one last 'I love you dearest. Don't ever forget your dear mother or me.'" The young woman planned to forget them. What good was a mother who was too weak to go on living and a father who thought an early life of scandal could later be redeemed through his daughter? She had been constantly reminded that she was a blessing undeserved by a man who had dedicated the first portion of his life to gambling and swindling and ill-gotten wealth. He had lost it all and had spent years rebuilding a career through legitimate means. The wife he married during those years had stuck with him through poverty and the long slow climb back to fortune. The daughter born to them had been a reward for clean living, but the father was ever aware of his past sins and how much he did not deserve to be blessed. The young woman was done hearing all the lessons he had learned from being ruined by living wild.

She changed out of her riding habit and into some proper grieving clothes. Entering the sick chamber, she stopped in her tracks. There, beside the bed, sat her father's lawyer. Her heart quickened as she thought that this certainly signaled the end was near. The lawyer vacated the chair beside the bed for her at once. Aware that she had an audience, she decided to make her act convincing.

"Father, I came as quickly as I could. You know how riding helps me think clearly. I'm not sure what I'm going to do when you're gone." She was conscious of the lawyer's steady gaze, so she forced a tear out of her eye and beckoned more to follow.

"Daughter, you know the kind of life I lived. I was immoral and unrestrained as a young man. You know how I was ruined. I've told you how I repented and how your good mother stood by me while I rebuilt a life. I haven't deserved any goodness or any fortune, for I was a bad one and ruined many other people in my early life."

"Yes, Father, but that's all in the past and you have more than made up for your wrong."

"No, Daughter, I haven't. Not yet. There's something I have left undone."

"Father, you can't be thinking of finding all the people you wronged. They were probably just as bad as you were. Don't dwell on things so far in the past."

"Not all the people. Just one person. There is one person I wronged, and before I die I have to make it right."

"Tell me who it is and I will tell that person whatever you say. I know you want to die with a clean conscience."

"You know I lived a wild life and didn't care who I hurt."

"Of course, but that doesn't matter now."

"I had a wife before your mother, and I left her."

The young woman had no response to this. The admission was completely new and she couldn't immediately discern how she would be affected.

"The wife I left has died." The young woman did not mean to, but she sighed audibly. The lawyer looked up suddenly from where he had been politely studying the floor during the conversation.

"However, my first wife and I had a baby."

"A baby! How could you be so…, and why wasn't I ever told!"

The father continued, ignoring the outburst, "The baby, of course, is a grown woman now, and I know where she is. I can't die until I have done right by her. She shouldn't have to suffer because of my misdeeds."

The young woman only heard, 'I can't die' and 'until I have done right.' One act was connected to the other in her father's speech. Deep in her heart she wanted her father to hurry up and end this ordeal, but now there was a dilemma of his doing right by someone who was a stranger, an unknown, a kin … a half-sister!

"Father, whoever she is and wherever she is, she has probably learned to cope with her lot in life. I'll write her a letter and tell her you are sorry for not being around, but that you are dying now, so all should be forgiven."

"No, my dearest. My soul cannot rest in peace until I have covered all my obligations."

Again, the young woman heard 'cannot rest in peace' and 'until …' She was becoming agitated at the thought that there existed someone of equal status as herself, though unknown, and that her father, judging by the presence of the lawyer, intended to do something with his will.

"My lawyer has already drafted a new will. I have just signed it today. But because you are my dearest, I wanted you to be prepared for the changes."

Real tears were flowing now from the young woman's eyes and they weren't tears of grief, unless you count what the woman felt over sharing her inheritance as grief.

"To follow my conscience and be fair, in my will I have stipulated that you will receive the farm and all the land."

"And the herd?" stammered the daughter.

"Yes," answered the father, "you will inherit the herd, but only half of it."

The eyes of the daughter were really stinging now. "How can you separate the herd?"

"I want my daughter, whom I didn't care for in life, to at least be blessed by my departing, and I want her to know that I am generous and a different man than the one who married her mother."

"Which half of the herd will you give her?"

"Aren't you interested in my going peacefully to my death with all my debts paid and nothing left undone?"

"Oh, I am, Father, but you know how attached I am to the horses. Will you cause me to suffer two blows, the first one of your death and the second one being separated from the herd?"

"Now, Daughter, I know you have your favorite horse, and I know you have a business sense. I feel sure you will be secure with the farm and half of the herd. You may certainly keep your Chestnut."

"Should I divide them? How will I decide? It will be painful."

"I have thought it all through, my dearest. To save you the pain, I have stipulated in my will that my first daughter, whom I neglected, will have free choice to select any half of the herd, except your Chestnut, and I have already purchased a smaller farm in the next county for her and the horses."

The young woman was speechless. This conversation had been too full of surprises. First, she had a half-sister, second, the half-sister was now going to inherit half of the horse herd, third, the half-sister would get to choose her half, fourth, her father had already bought that woman a farm, and fifth, the lawyer was watching her too closely and had witnessed the whole conversation. It would be impossible to claim her father had lost possession of his senses.

The distraught daughter needed to leave the room to think through how to deal with this most unfortunate wrinkle. To excuse herself she said, "Father, don't overexert yourself. Rest now."

He indeed was ready to rest. His eternal rest was upon him now that he had covered all his obligations. As his daughter shut the door on her way out, he shut his eyes, not to open them again. Only the lawyer witnessed his passing.

When the sad news was announced, the young woman executed her plan to show no weakness and to immediately take charge. The funeral was managed and the mourning was accomplished and the old man was laid to rest on a hill overlooking the horse farm, although the daughter had wanted him to be buried at the cemetery to put some distance between him and her. Then all the household and farm staff were called together by the lawyer for the reading of the will.

There were sniffles and sighs and murmurings as the will was read out, beginning from the least amount bequeathed to loyal stable hands and household staff, to the greatest amount left to the two daughters. At the mention of a second daughter, a great noise of surprise erupted, but the young woman showed all signs of equanimity and prior knowledge. Contributing to her steady bearing was the scheme that she had settled on the night before. Therefore, she confidently inquired of the lawyer, "When will my half-sister be coming to select her half of the herd?"

The lawyer replied that she had been notified of her inheritance prior to the old man's death, according to his wishes, and that she would be coming in three days.

The young woman looked around at the group gathered in the room and said, "Don't you think Father would be pleased if we treated her to a meal in the formal dining room and asked her to stay overnight?" With a large measure of surprise, they all agreed.

The half-sister arrived in the evening as scheduled and was welcomed with polite words and formal manners by the new mistress of the farm. The two sat at opposite ends of the long oak table and were served in elegant style. The new mistress of the farm spoke with passion about their deceased father's intense struggle to rebuild his life and fortune after being ruined, and the key part the horse herd had played in it. At first, her father had been laughed at. Everyone assumed he had lost his mind along with his fortune when he hastily bought a small heard of unkempt and sickly horses about to be sent to the glue factory. Of course, the wealth of the herd was not in its condition or size but in its blood. When foals were born to some of these and they fetched sums beyond imagination, the laughs were quickly silenced. She praised her father's shrewd business sense and boasted that he had groomed her to carry on the vision. The half-sister appeared uneasy with the conversation and remained quiet.

As the new mistress of the farm sized up her half-sister during the meal, she supposed that the half-sister's unease implied greed, and her silence covered deception. She assumed that since her father had lived a wild and unethical life when the half-sister was born, that those same characteristics were inherited, just as the half-sister was now inheriting half of the horse herd. Therefore her scheme would work, she concluded.

The half-sister was some years older than the new mistress of the horse farm. Though she hadn't known her father, she hadn't resented being fatherless. When she was contacted about his last will and testament, she accepted the terms as a rightful daughter, but she had no desire to gain anything during her time at the horse farm except the half that she had inherited. Since she had already chosen to make her way in the world by raising hunting dogs, the idea of raising horses was all the more appealing. However, she was never asked during the meal what it was she did as an occupation, and she did not offer it unbidden.

With the formal meal over, the young mistress of the farm suggested that dividing the herd could best be done in the light of the next day. The half-sister agreed and was shown to the guestroom that faced away from the horse pasture. The equestrian ribbons and trophies that adorned the room had all been recently dusted and polished.

Even though her father's will prevented his younger daughter from choosing the horses she would keep, she had her preferences. Needless to say, these were the strongest and the ones of the purest strains. There were twenty-four horses in the herd, not counting her Chestnut, so she selected the twelve that would give her the best offspring when breeding was done. Since the half-sister would select her half by sight (without being able to examine their pedigree papers), the young mistress had decided to mar the appearance, but not permanently, of the horses she desired to keep, assuming that the half-sister would naturally choose only those which appeared perfect.

In the deepest part of the night, the young mistress went out into the pasture where all the horses were standing. Some had sheltered under feeding sheds, and some were on the far side under their favorite trees. She begged each horse's understanding and forgiveness as she carried out her plan, for the beauty of the horse was still the only thing that touched her heart.

The next day as she stood by the pasture fence with the half-sister, she carried on a monologue about the names of each horse, their characteristics, and identified the ones she had learned to ride on. The half-sister interrupted her suddenly.

"I have decided. There's no need to give any further information."

"Really?" asked the young mistress, "Don't you want to look in their mouths and check their fetlocks?"

"No, I've quite decided, and I'll be ready to load them onto the wagons immediately."

"You really surprise me. I certainly don't want you to feel rushed when you can take more time to decide."

"I feel quite certain. There are a particular twelve horses that I want, and it will be easy for the stable hands to identify them without their names." The young mistress knew her plan had worked.

"I want the twelve horses which are limping."

The new mistress of the farm paled and gulped. The half-sister had done exactly the opposite of what she had expected. She had counted on the half-sister choosing as she would have chosen.

The half-sister continued, "I am fond of animals, and I have a special concern for any which are lame or suffering. That's how I've made my living, but up till now only with hounds. I take them in and rehabilitate them, if possible. If not, I just give them a home."

With no further discussion, the half-sister gladly took the lame half of the herd, feeling satisfied that she was doing a good turn for the new young mistress by leaving her the means to fulfill their father's vision.

It was not until she had settled the lame twelve on her new farm that she discovered the cause of their misery — sharp objects inserted into their hooves. She removed the objects, and thereby restored their beauty. As things turned out, she was the one to truly carry on the father's vision – redeeming the marred and fallen with hand and heart.

♪

The Kitchen

Evil controls through anger.
Love sometimes gets burned.

One day the Kitchen decided to leave the house. Can you imagine — leave the house!?! It was already out of town when I caught up and asked, "Where are you going with the dishes and cups? Are you upset?"

Of course, the Kitchen didn't reply, but the oven, puffing smoke, bellowed a cry, "We're tired. Just tired. That's all. So when the Kitchen said go, we answered the call and went. Gruff-Huff-Poof!"

"But," I protested, "you've so many meals and holidays and birthdays and parties and ... and so many occasions provided for. How can you all that success ignore?"

The oven shut its door and frowned. The teapot pouted its lip and looked down, "He said tired. We're all just tired."

Upon hearing that, I naïvely inquired, "Tired of What?"

You'd think I had tickled a laughing hyena! The shrieks from the pots and the pans and the china, the flatware and sink and the Kitchen itself, revealed very clearly the anger they felt! Then up flared the stove and the cutlery flew and I barely escaped, and I now must tell you — whoever enters a hot Kitchen nave exceeds and surpasses the bravest of brave. And I, for one, I tell you my friend, shall not ever question a Kitchen again.

Furniture Talk

Evil orchestrates its surroundings. Love embraces them.

"Hey, you, Queen Anne Chair & Hassock, quit that twittering gossip. I'm in charge now that the people have left."

"What! You in charge? What makes you so sure?"

"Humph! Of course I'm in charge. Who do you think was just sitting in me? The master of the house, naturally, and that means I'm the master of the sitting room."

"Well, excuse me, Mr. Slipcovered Armchair, but the madam of the house was just sitting in me, and it appears to me that she is the one in charge."

"I'll have you know that I have been in this sitting room longer than anyone, and I'll thank you to call me Sir."

"… Sir? …"

"Who's that?"

"It's me, the Grandfather Clock. I believe I was standing right here the day they brought you in. You were wearing a different covering then, heh, heh, heh. But I was standing right here, ticking away and making my chimes."

"What is this, a conspiracy? So they gave me a slipcover. That's because I'm so important. They had to make me a new coat to keep my stuffing in since I get sat in a lot by the master of the house. Did you hear that? The master of the house sits in me, and no one else."

"Ho, ho! So you got a new coat. That still doesn't make you older than I am, does it?

"Look, Grandpa Clock, I was speaking to the pieces of furniture as make up the sitting room. I don't notice that you're getting sat on. Why don't you just keep your ticktocks to yourself and quit chiming in when I'm trying to talk."

"Uh-hum, excuse me, Mr. Armchair, it's time for my nap."

"Mr. Over-Stuffed Armchair, can we take a nap or do we need your permission?"

"Queen Anne & Hassock, I've had about enough of your insolence. I don't care what you do, so long as you don't twitter and shake the foundations of this sitting room. I've got to rest up for the next time the master comes to sit in me."

"I think the Hassock and I'll get the master to try us out next time."

"Don't you dare. I'm his chair and I've always been his chair."

"Well, we don't think you deserve to be his chair. He's kind and thoughtful and you're an old brute."

"Now, look here. If it wasn't for me, there wouldn't even be a sitting room. Look how all of you are positioned around me. Obviously, I am the most important chair in this room and you have no right to insult me."

"Please, excuse me, but beggin' your pardon, Mr. Armchair…"

"What are you creaking about, Miss Sofa?"

"Well, I might be wrong, but, well, aren't we all important in our own way?"

"I wouldn't go gettin' too uppity, Miss Sofa. You may get sat on a lot by those three rambunctious kids, but if you were really important, the people would replace your springs when you creak like you've been doing lately."

"Mr. Armchair, that is a very unkind thing to say to Miss Sofa. She has the most difficult job of any of us, and it's not nice of you to make light of her ailments."

"Listen, Queen Anne, didn't I say I didn't want to hear anything more out of you? I'm in charge here, and it's my job to let the rest of you know where you stand in the order of things."

"But, Mr. Armchair, beggin' your pardon again, they wanted to replace my springs a long time ago, but it would have meant destroying my covering, and they couldn't do that, as it matches the drapes."

"Good point, Miss Sofa! And please notice, Mr. Rag-Bag Armchair, that you don't even match your old upholstery. Your tatty old leg is showing."

"Queen Anne, if I have to, I'll come over there and give you a kick in your leg to shut you up."

"You don't scare me, Mr. Too-Big-for-Your-Britches. You couldn't move if you worked at it all day. Now me, I'm as agile as the day I was brought here. The madam sits in me whenever she's tired, and she gets up saying how good she feels after resting in my cushion. I know I'm important. You're just a grumpy old lump of stuffing."

"Ouch! Ouch!"

"Who's that?"

"It's me, Mr. Armchair — the Carpet. That hurts me when you try to move like that."

"When did you get there? I never saw you before."

"They brought me in when the weather got cold, and you've all been standing on me keeping your feet warm."

"Humph! I could scoot over to Sassy Queen Anne and give her a bark on the shins if you weren't there."

"But I am here, and you're hurting me. Can't you stay still?"

"Who are you to talk to me like that? I'm the master's chair and I can do whatever I want in this sitting room. I am the most important."

"Please, don't be offended, Mr. Armchair, but I heard the madam say on the day she rolled me out that I really brought the whole room together and made it feel cozy and warm. And don't forget that the master does rest his feet on me."

"Oh, no you don't! You can't claim to have the master's authority just because he puts his feet on you. I've got my feet on you just now, and how does that make you feel?"

"Ouch! You're hurting me."

"Mr. Armchair, if you don't quit hurting the Carpet, I'm gonna ... well, I'm gonna have to do something about it."

"You! What can you do to me, Mr. Lanky Floor Lamp?"

"I may not look strong, but I have something in me that could leap out and make it get pretty hot for you."

"Oh, ho! You electric Lamps might be brilliant, but you haven't got any brains. Did it ever occur to you that if you try to burn me up you might also make it hot for the precious Carpet! I tell you, if you send one spark at me, the whole room goes up. Try that one on for size, Mr. Floor Lamp Without-a-Brain."

"Really, Mr. Heavy Armchair, you are too much. Do you think you can be the boss in here when all you do is insult the rest of us?"

"Queen Anne, I haven't even started to insult you yet. I'm just trying to remind this frail tube of electricity and this thin layer of wool and that box of squeaking springs that I am in charge because the master sits in me, and that makes it final. If everyone would just agree that I am in charge, I wouldn't be forced to speak the truth."

"Boy, I wish the maid would come in."

"Now who's that talking and saying silly things?"

"Hey, don't mind me. As I see it, Mr. Armchair, since I don't get sat on, I'm not really part of your problem. I'm just the Hutch and I have an itch. If the maid would just come in and give me a good dusting, that would scratch it. But since I've overheard your discussion, I might mention that I'm pretty important myself. Not only am I made of cherry wood, but I hold all the crystal and china and silver."

"Humph! And does the master ever have anything to do with you, or just the women folk? I tell you, that no one else can claim the master like I can, and in his absence, I am the most important."

"Hey, I don't want to argue with you, I itch too bad. Besides that, my hinges need a good stretch. Usually that maid has come in by now. I wonder what's keeping her."

"Did you hear that, Mr. Males-Only Armchair? Some in this room don't care if you insult them. They know their worth, and they don't need some fatso to be their boss."

"Queen Anne, your legs look like good kindling for the fireplace. I've got more brawn on my one arm than you have head to toe. Why don't you shut up and let those of us with more substantial frames do the talking!"

"Well, I never, in all my days have met with such an audacious, self-aggrandizing piece of furniture as yourself. I hope I get moved to the madam's bedroom so I don't have to sit in your presence any longer."

"Delivery man here. Sir, where do you want me to put your new armchair?"

"Right there where the old one is sitting will be fine. You can take the old one away, and you might as well burn it. It's not worth saving."

"Help! Someone help me!"

"A-hem. What a splendid looking sitting room I have just been placed in. Allow me to introduce myself. I am William Armchair the Third. You can call me Wills. And who might this lovely Queen Anne be? And such an elegant Sofa. The drapes bring out your best colour, Madam. And my, oh, my, the Carpet certainly is a cushion for my sore feet! And who might this tall gallant fellow be behind me? I'm sure we'll all get on splendidly."

♪

A Highland Lament

Evil selfishly lies. Love selflessly gives.

Baron von Dael was a very greedy man, a very greedy man indeed; but he hid his naughty vice from the foolish and the wise by tithing all his wealth religiously. But beyond this tepid token of his generosity, the Baron never helped another soul. Still, the Baron always said, "I pray the poor are fed!" and "Fortune for myself is not the goal! O no! Fortune for myself is *not* a goal!"

Now, the Preacher and the Doc and the Mayor and the Cop were indebted to the Baron for their pay, so the Baron called on them to be sure he'd always win if a threat should ever dare to cross his way.

It is thus that poor Gus does now enter in this tale, for he made a food that very magic'ly has the power in itself to multiply itself, so the buyer buys it once and then is free. Free! Yes, O free from the pain of hunger's grip and free from sudden bell that death does ring. But for Baron von Dael who does make his wealth through sale of costly food that's processed by machine, the invention of poor Gus caused a mighty rotten fuss in his profit-making fine food industry.

So the Baron did begin with fervor fast to spin a web of sticky lies, and here they be:

The Cop said, "Gus is shady!" as the Doc said, "He is crazy!" while the Mayor said, "That Gus I cannot trust!" Then the Preacher filled the air with a holy, reverent prayer, "O dear Lord please keep such *poison* far from us!"

By the time that all these lies were thus sounded through the skies, the food that Gus was making caused a scare! So the food and recipe were both burned for all to see and poor Gus was sent forever far from there.

But in a far-off land where the people lend a hand to anyone who travels in their way, Gus freely sold his food, and that nation quickly grew to be the very most ingenious of that day.

Baron von Dael was a very greedy man, a very greedy man indeed; though he hid his naughty vice, Highland folk put him on ice when they read this selfsame story that you read. The moral of this tale is not one that I can tell, but here's the reason Baron's in his tomb:

> Danger surely looms
> when a poet's in the room
> because funny words on paper spell out doom,
> sometimes;
> yes, funny words on paper spelled *his* doom.

☙

Feather Quills

Evil keeps charity in its place. Love surprises.

Once upon a time there was a family — a father, a mother, an older sister, a middle brother, and a younger brother. They lived a happy life in a pleasant house and got along together in a most agreeable way. It was a fairy tale life.

The father was quite rich. He had made his money in a diamond mine as a young man and had returned to live a life of ease in his home country. The mother was beautiful and smart and enjoyed her life, keeping herself busy by painting with oils on canvas. The daughter was also beautiful and could play the piano and sing. The middle son was very intelligent, and a private tutor was engaged to educate him. The youngest son was gentle and playful. He loved animals.

Now the family had no problems that they knew of. The father made a job out of managing his money. The mother occupied herself in creating and selling her masterpieces. The daughter found herself desired by many local young men. She could have her pick of any as a husband. The middle son devoted himself to his studies and was likely to become a great lawyer. The youngest son was too young for schooling and he busied himself all day among his small farm of animals.

Among his menagerie was a lamb, a pony, a rabbit, and a goose. In all his waking hours he was employed in putting out their food, cleaning their stalls, combing their fur, and carrying on the most wonderful conversations. It seems most unlikely, but it is true, that of all his animals, he loved the goose the most. The goose was the only animal in his collection that needed neither a stall cleaned nor a coat brushed. The boy couldn't do anything for the goose except toss down his corn each morning. Yet, he enjoyed the goose more than all the other pets.

The boy went about all his chores with the goose ever at his heels. While he brushed his pony, the goose was there waddling about between his legs. When he cleaned out the hutch of his rabbit, the goose was there to keep him company. The goose even helped the boy clean the burrs out of the lamb's woolly coat.

As well as things were between the goose and the boy, they were not so well between the goose and the other members of this happy and contented family. The goose had only good manners around the boy. Yet, whenever any other member of the family came too near, the goose flew at them with an outstretched neck, and if he got near enough to them before they ran away, he gave them a painful peck. The family members kindly implored the younger brother to curb the behavior of the goose, but the young fellow was unable to understand how the goose was so tame around him and so ferocious around everyone else. He only knew how to care for his animals and never had any cause to guide their behavior. Besides, all of his animals got along well together. There was never so much as a spat inside his animal pen.

The boy was sorry that his mother and father and sister and brother couldn't appreciate the goose as much as he could, but he was just a small boy and he continued to love the goose anyway.

One day the boy was obliged to visit his grandmother who lived a full day's coach ride away. He had been loathe to leave his animals, but his grandmother had been asking for a long time for him to come, and she could not understand that a boy so young would not be free to provide his grandmother with some company. So the boy packed a small bag and reluctantly bid farewell to his coterie of furry and feathered friends. While he was gone, the members of his family assured him that they would feed and look after his animals.

The goose was really bad. If the goose had not been so bad he might still be alive today, but he was so bad that all the members of the boy's family got pecked and chased and honked at and in other ways humiliated. Granted, the goose missed the boy and probably figured in his goose's heart that the family members were keeping him away. How was a goose supposed to understand about grandmothers who want young grandsons to keep them company?

When the boy returned, he was met by all of his family with the bad news that the goose had wreaked havoc. They had all tried to enter the animal pen to feed the other animals only to have the goose attack them here and there on their bodies. The mother tried first, but she suffered a wounded hand. The sister tried after that, and she had her best dress torn and her leg pecked. The brother was sure he could do better, but he got nipped in the back of the pants, and as a result, couldn't sit down properly. The father finally came in to get the job done, but he got chased all around the pasture until he tripped over a stump. His arm was in a sling.

The young son was very sad to hear about the bad behavior of his goose and he wished he hadn't gone to visit his grandmother. He was just about to promise that he would never go away again and leave his goose to wreak havoc when the whole family insisted that the goose be killed and eaten at the holiday which was coming up. The boy was so stricken with the thought that he dashed out to his animal pen and threw his arms around his goose and cried into his feathers. The boy couldn't understand how such a tame goose could be so nasty.

The boy was very obedient to his parents and he loved his sister and his brother as well. Although he loved his goose, he knew that it was wrong for an animal to inflict wounds onto well-meaning caretakers. So the next day, the goose was killed, plucked, dressed, and made ready for the pot. The feathers of the goose were reserved by the boy so that he could remember his beloved, but naughty goose. Everyone in the family admired the courage of their youngest member and vowed to replace the goose with a more amiable duck.

The goose, however, wasn't completely finished with the family. You might say he was a magic goose because, although he was dead and ready to be eaten alongside potatoes and corn and other good food, part of him was going to go on living.

No one could have known (since it is a rather complex phenomenon) that the family was not really living as happily and contentedly as outward appearances might suggest. The father was rich and had a life of ease just managing his fortune. The mother was free to paint and enjoy her children. The sister's hand was sought by numerous wealthy and eligible men. The middle brother was a commendable scholar and had a promising future. But the truth is, only the youngest brother was doing completely as he wished. He was fortunate to be young and unencumbered by convention. All the other members of his family were in various ways burdened by doing right things in the right way, all the while secretly wishing they could be doing something else, but they were afraid to try.

This is where the life of the goose comes in, as you will soon see. By the end, I'm sure you will concede that he was, after all, a magic goose, and you will wonder if he didn't misbehave so thoroughly the day his little master was away just so he could find himself in a cooking pot and his feathers made into quills.

The goose bequeathed some very fine quills from his tail feathers to the family. They were ideal for making into pens because they could be sharpened into nice points. No one took much notice that it was the goose's feathers that were now being put into service as quill pens. It was the young boy who had independently decided that he would prepare a selection of them in order to further the life of his pet goose.

Just as the goose did not behave toward the family members, so now his tail feathers were going to cause mischief. Whenever any of the family members (except the youngest boy) picked up a quill to write a letter, something very unexpected came out onto the paper. It wasn't that they weren't thinking of what they wrote, but they were making an effort to write the message that was expected instead of what they really wanted. However, when they saw what the quill pen wrote, they recognized it as the thought they were thinking but didn't dare to put down on paper. Even if they tried again on a new piece of paper, it came out the same. Their hidden thought came out onto the paper and their conventional thought was left inside their head. They never suspected the quill pens. They, of course, never thought of the goose, either.

When they couldn't get the more conventional thought to appear on the paper, they stopped to wonder, for the first time, if they should perhaps go ahead and take the risk that was before them. Each of them, in turn, had their own experience with one of the goose's quill pens. And this is what happened.

The mother seemed content as an artist, sitting in the meadow, putting each new scene onto canvas. But when she sat down to write a letter to ask for a new delivery of oils and canvas, she found herself writing instead for a delivery of cloth and thread. It was not until she had written out the whole letter that she realized the cloth and thread could be used to make clothes for the growing number of displaced persons in their region. She tried over and over again to write the letter that would sustain her leisurely hobby, but it kept coming out as asking for supplies that would turn her efforts into charity. Finally, she sent the letter and didn't tell anyone about her emerging conviction.

When the daughter picked up her quill pen, it was to write a secret letter to a man who was asking for her hand in marriage. He wasn't one of the "eligible" ones. He was a poor musician and he was planning to make a trip to a faraway country. The daughter privately adored him more than any of the other suitors, but she hadn't been able to accept his offer because as the daughter of a rich man she should naturally marry within her social status.

When she picked up the quill, she meant to profess to care for him, yet refuse him for the third time. Instead, she wrote a love letter of the most endearing sort and offered to elope with him that very night and travel all over the world with him as his wife. Several times she took a new piece of paper and tried to write a refusal, but since only her true feelings came pouring forth from the quill, she decided it must be the right thing to do.

Next, in a quiet moment, the studious son picked up his quill. His aim had been to write to a prestigious law firm in the capital city, seeking a post as a legal assistant. What came out from that clever quill was a letter to a medical school asking for admittance so he could train to be a doctor among the coal miners. He found the pen writing all manner of diseases which were a bane to miners and their families, and he saw his own hand declare that he wanted to help cure the diseases and improve life for the miners. He, of course, rewrote his letter again and again but to no avail. At last, he sealed his letter and sent it off without a word to anyone, least of all his father who had expressed hope that his son would become his legal advisor in regard to the family wealth.

Next came the father's turn. He approached his quill much as he had approached the goose that day. Bold and sure of himself, he sat at his desk to engineer a new plan to grow his money by leaps and bounds. The letter he wrote was to his banker. He had intended to give detailed instructions about the buying and selling of certain of his holdings. To his surprise, he wrote, via the quill, that he wanted a large portion of his money to be used among the poor of the largest city. He shook his head violently as he tried again to write a proper letter of financial instructions to his banker. But, again and again, instructions for using his money to improve the lives of the poverty stricken kept coming out, and each time he wrote the letter, the figure got bigger and bigger and the program became more and more ambitious. Eventually he sealed and sent his letter, too.

You can imagine how the goose was chuckling. All on one day, the lives of the family changed drastically. The daughter was found missing the next morning, and no one would have known where she was except for all the copies of the letters which were left lying about. To the family's utter amazement, when the mother received her shipment, it was bolts of cloth instead of painting supplies. She at once began to sew. The son packed away his law books and began reading in medicine. The father began to take an interest in the city slums and made frequent trips there to see how conditions could be improved.

Only the youngest son went on as he did before. He cleaned the stalls of his animals and combed out their coats and took care that they had enough food. One day the mother looked up from her sewing and remarked at how changed the family was. She wondered out loud how all these changes had come about.

The changes also caused the youngest son to wonder what he would do when he grew up. He gave the matter serious thought, and then told his mother that he would have a goose farm and make feather quills.

♪

GOOD QUEEN JILL

Evil cannot abide idealism. Love believes all things.

There once was a tower where sat a good Queen, but just through a window was she ever seen. Her goodness made bishops and princes all fear to ever let her to her people draw near. They feared that she'd give all their riches away and cancel the taxes the poor had to pay.

"Queen Jill, don't you see that the poor need the rich, 'cos their little wagons need some place to hitch. They can't afford horses or stables or barns; 'tis better if they do the work on our farms."

Queen Jill didn't say what she had in her mind — she knew that their cunning was hard to unwind. So later that night when the castle was dark and no one expected the Queen to depart, Queen Jill stole away under cover of night disguised in a peasant cape, tied and held tight. Into the shadows of village she crept and into the square where a woman she met did tell her to hurry and get off the streets 'cos shadows will swallow a wench's bare feet. But seeing her feet fit in finest of shoes, the elderly lady there started to coo, "And what have we here on the street all alone — does seem like the lady has lost her way home! How much do you want, Dearie, for those fine hoofs?"

Before the Queen mustered her thoughtful reply, two sets of strong hands seemed to come from the sky to yank her from danger and take her back home – t'were guards of the Bishop who'd seen the Queen roam.

"Queen Jill, you are twenty," the Bishop did say. "You certainly shall be a Saint if you pray for all of the lost ones who wander in dark. So come now, Milady, it's time you embark upon quiet pilgrimage 'cross the blue sea."

And thus our Queen Jill did get lost in history.

The Ferryboat Puller

Evil hates and divides. Love connects and restores.

No one had ever crossed it. There was no bridge. The river was wide, and running right down the middle of it was a curtain of fog. The fog always hung there and completely obscured the view from one bank to the other.

On one side of the river lived a people who could go where they pleased. They were naturally fond of travel and discovery as long as it didn't take them over water. They called their land Sunland because the sun always shone. On the Other Side of the river lived a people who were not able to travel so freely. These people adored their land even though it wasn't a land of perpetual sunshine. Neither side knew much about the other because the fog never lifted to give a clear view.

Without a bridge there was no way to cross, so the opposite sides of the river made up stories about the other. They were such awful stories that at the end of them everyone shivered and said, "I'm glad there isn't a bridge. Otherwise, the other side might come over and destroy us."

One day the people on both sides were surprised to find that a ferryboat had been installed. No one was sure where it had come from, but the man on board had a most ingenious way of working his ferry. A cable stretched the width of the river and by pulling hand over hand with wooden grips, the ferryboat man pulled the ferry from one side to the other.

Now at first, while he sat docked on the Sunland shore, the people asked him about the people on the Other Side. He simply replied, "The people over there are hearty. They have a beauty deeper than a tan." No one could imagine what he meant.

The people on the Sunland side noticed that the ferryboat puller sometimes came through the fog soaking wet, or sometimes with a sunburn, and still again, with snow still clinging to his shoulders and his hair. When they asked him about this peculiarity, he accurately reported that the weather on the Other Side changes quite often and one must be prepared for anything.

The ferryboat puller went back and forth across the river. The Sunlanders watched him from the bank and could see him only until he went into the curtain of fog which ran down the middle of the river. When he was lost from view, and as they turned away, they remarked that they hoped he survived the trip across the water and whatever awaited him on the other bank. They still believed that the Other Side was really populated by savages.

One day the ferryboat puller brought back a beautiful lily — the likes of which the people in Sunland had never seen. This one lily, a simple flower of unusual color, was enough for a few of the Sunlanders to give up their fear of water and their suspicions. They said it was doubtful that barbarians could grow such a lily. Their inbred curiosity to see new places began to surge, and a few privately approached the ferryboat puller to see if he would take them across.

This is precisely what the ferryboat puller had hoped would happen. He knew the old suspicions could never die unless the two sides of the riverbank could see each other. So he agreed to take them across. Just before the Sunlanders stepped on board, they had a moment of hesitation. They suddenly remembered that sometimes the ferryboat puller emerged from the fog bank dripping wet, or worse yet, wearing snow. They only knew sunshine and were deathly afraid of any condition that clouded the sun. So they asked the puller if he got wet inside the fog or on the Other Side. The puller told them plainly that the sun did not always shine on the Other Side, but with proper apparel they could shield themselves from the elements and see for themselves where the beautiful lily grew.

The apprehensions of the first people to cross helped them to be prepared — they carried with them not only an umbrella, but also a pair of boots and a long coat with a hood. When the ferryboat went into the fog bank and the slurping of the water under the ferry was all that they could hear, they had a moment of pure fear and they distrusted the ferryboat puller and were sure that they had been duped into danger. All thoughts of the lily were swept from their minds as they considered ways to get the ferryboat going back to the Sunland side. Just before they could act, however, the ferry emerged from the fog bank and the passengers from Sunland found themselves gazing on a wonderland of new sights. Such was their wonder as they embarked onto the land that they scarcely said goodbye to the ferryboat puller.

After some Sunlanders had gone to the Other Side and come back safely, there was increased interest from other Sunlanders. They were intrigued by the lilies that were brought back and were eager to see them growing in their native soil. The old superstitions and the fear of water were all but forgotten. The line of those waiting to cross on the ferry grew and grew.

Various accounts were given about the weather by those who had gone and returned. Some said they had taken all the proper gear only to need none of it. Others said they had used every bit of what they had taken, and if they hadn't taken boots, for instance, they would've suffered frostbite. Still others said an umbrella would suffice, and anything else was superfluous.

Those who waited upon the banks of Sunland for their turn to be carried across discussed what they had heard about the weather on the Other Side. Sometimes tempers flared as accounts of the weather differed. Standing in line, each predicted the type of weather that would be found on his or her journey, feeling like meteorological experts just by knowing a few new weather words. Some were afraid of anything but sun. They predicted their visit would be during a sunny period. Some were curious about snow. They expected their visit to coincide with a snowfall.

To settle the disagreement, someone asked the ferryboat puller what the weather had been like when he left the Other Side. He was willing to tell them, but he cautioned that it changed quite often. He couldn't predict what it would be like on the next trip. But since Sunlanders had no experience with anything except constant sunshine, they gave no importance to his caution about changeable weather.

The ferryboat puller could not help but notice a change in the passengers. They were no longer the ones who gladly came prepared for any kind of weather. These passengers wanted to know about the weather in advance so that they could leave unnecessary gear behind. The first time the puller was sure that he was carrying a different breed of passenger was when a young Sunlander came through the fog bank into a sunny day, and with his unnecessary umbrella, hit the ferryboat puller over the head. That same fellow had a fabulous time. But in spite of this, on his return trip, he saw no need to apologize for his rudeness.

The next passenger left all her gear on the banks of Sunland because the puller had said it was sunny when he left the Other Side, though he again cautioned that it might change. When she came through the fog bank and saw heavy snow falling, she demanded that the puller give up his coat and boots to her so that she wouldn't miss her adventure. When he refused, she called him all sorts of names and threatened to report him as a scoundrel.

The next passenger and the next and the next were all of the same sort. If something didn't go the way they planned regarding the weather, they either beat the ferryboat puller with their umbrellas or tried to take his gear. One Sunlander even blamed the puller for his own troubles on land when, instead of paying for them, he had stolen some of the lilies.

The ferryboat puller was almost sorry that he had set up his ferry, and yet, he was satisfied that the old superstitious stories about each bank of the river were never told anymore. Everyone in Sunland not only had seen a lily from the Other Side, they had one of their own, and so many of the Sunlanders had loved the feel of snow that they had invented a way to make it in Sunland. The ferryboat puller had done the job he had set out to do even if he wasn't appreciated for it.

But one day, he came out of the fog bank and saw the waiting crowd on the Sunland side, all of them tapping their umbrellas impatiently and jostling to be nearer to the front. Just then, he gave in to his instincts. He went back into the fog, cut his cable, and floated away.

To this day, the Sunlanders never tire of recounting the irresponsible way the ferryboat puller left them standing on the riverbank. In each telling, he becomes more and more of a scoundrel. Now that there is a bridge between the two sides of the river, no one even remembers that he and his ferry were the first bridge. Instead, he is remembered solely for not being able to predict the weather on the Other Side and for cutting his cable, leaving them in the lurch.

Soon after the puller had cut his cable, a rumor surfaced that as he floated away that day his ferry had turned into a chariot pulled by fiery horses which, as it soared upwards, burned away the curtain of fog. But that rumor was started by a young child who surely couldn't have known anything. At any rate, his departure exactly coincided with the lifting of the fog.

♪

We'll Die Without Pizza!

Evil demands satiated appetites. Love is temperate.

Coming home, the family of mice searched through their cupboards for something nice; but finding there nothing savory or sweet, the family of mice all stamped their feet: "We've gotta go find ourselves something to eat!"

The family then sped to the kitchen above and together indulged in their greatest love. Inside the cardboard which lay on the table, they stuffed their mouths full with all they were able. First gnawing and crunching, then munching it down, the mice were attacking a pizza they found. But then, suddenly, a light lit up the room and they were all trapped in their cardboard tomb. The family of people all leapt up and down, smushing the mice with a squishy cheese sound.

Losing their food made them irate and starved: "We'll die without pizza! Quick, out to the car!"

'Twas hunger that drove them to speed on their way. The cop stopping them said, "Ya should've obeyed that red light back there, 'cos now you must pay!"

The fine was so much that their hunger increased which drove them to eat and to eat and to eat. They ate so much pizza they died in their sleep. So next time you're hungry and stomp with your feet, beware of the fate that these stompers did meet!

The First Fairy

Love overpowers evil.

A long time ago when the world was more wicked and people were more selfish and tempers rose higher and fists flew more quickly, there were no fairies. It's not that fairies weren't needed; they were just unknown.

Back then, the one who received all the respect was the one who knocked others out of the way, always pushed to the front of the line, took what belonged to others, and grew red in the face uttering curses. This may sound strange to us now since we live in a time when wickedness isn't a virtue, but that's how it was then.

You wouldn't expect anyone to wear a smile in those days or to sing a merry song or to share their bread with another or to help someone else with their work. These things were never done. Even a mother and father had no feeling for their own children. All the brows were knit, all the mouths were frowning, all the eyes were shifty, and all the fists were twitching. Mistrust was the most acceptable home atmosphere, and all the best families excelled in it.

You might shiver when you hear that a little girl was born to one such family with seven older brothers. The brothers were all experts in mistrusting each other. When it came time to eat, they each tried to win the other's admiration by grabbing the most food. When it came time to sleep, the praise went to the one who took all the covers, making the others freeze. The mother and father of this brood were quite pleased by the actions of their sons, but of course, they didn't show their pleasure by smiling and hugging the sons. Instead, they knit their brows more fiercely and sent their own fists flying in all directions as they dove to get the most food for themselves. They acted the same way with the covers at night, and that is how the sons learned the right way to sleep.

The little girl was born and everyone was so very displeased. You might wonder how these wicked people would show their displeasure if they showed their pleasure by frowning. It was quite a sight to see. They were each embarrassed when it happened. In fact, they quickly covered it up with their own more comfortable faces. The baby girl had been laid on a bed, and whenever anyone looked at her fresh, tender face, they felt a very strange convulsion in their cheeks. It just happened without their knowing it. It hurt like a blow to the face, and besides, it made them feel suddenly unprepared to be wicked and selfish. It was a smile. To stop the pains in their faces, the seven brothers suddenly held up their fists as if to fight, and that returned their old faces to them.

In those days, names were chosen with utmost care since people saw it as a supreme virtue to live up to their given names. As you might guess, the most popular names were Stupid, Dumbo, Dingbat, Dunce, Filthy-rat, Noodle-brain, and Dimwit — names we would never consider calling someone today. But because the little girl so displeased her mother and father, they refused to give her a respectable name. And since any alternative names were too repugnant, the little girl just went nameless.

Things only got worse as she grew. She wasn't developing like a normal child. As she would sit in a corner and chew on toys, she made the most disgusting cooing noises when anyone came into the room. Her arms would flap up and down, and she would kick her little feet, and worst of all, she would smile. The mother and the father worried that she didn't have a temper.

Since the little girl made the family so uncomfortable, they tried to look at her as little as possible because that funny thing happened to their cheeks whenever they did. When the boys came in from fighting and were looking for their meal, they did their best to not look in her direction. However, she would trick them with her sudden laughing sounds, and they would turn their heads involuntarily, and then — the worst — they would smile. She was too little to fight them at mealtime, but while they were all a flurry of fists and curses trying to get the most, the little unnamed girl would laugh and flap her arms and kick her little feet. To get her to stop this rude behavior, the brothers would offer her a bit of their own bread. It generally worked. She loved to eat and couldn't laugh with bread in her mouth.

Life went on in this family and they tried to keep the character of their youngest member a secret from the rest of the people. After all, they had a reputation to keep up of being regarded as the most wicked, the most selfish, the most tempestuous, and the fastest to the punch. However, when the little girl began to walk and talk, her parents realized it was time for her to learn to get on in the world. They thought she needed to be around other children in order to learn the proper ways of acting.

The little unnamed girl was sent to play among other small children, and the very same thing happened as happened to her seven brothers. As she could talk now and not just gurgle and coo, the kindness of her words along with that funny look on her face and especially that gentle laugh, made all the other small children experience pains in their faces. They even stopped punching each other and stealing each other's toys because when their cheeks slid up instead of down, they had to stop and feel them. All the time that the little girl was among them, they looked very strange indeed. They held their hands to their faces and they tipped their heads from side to side to see if they could make their cheeks go down. One unfortunate boy accidentally let out a little laugh that sounded just like the one the unnamed girl had made. He got thumped on the back of the head by his mother, so he never laughed again.

The little girl continued to grow but never became like the rest of the people. The brothers even tried to put on demonstrations for how to be selfish and how to fight and how to curse, but their efforts never seemed to sink into the girl's skull. They found themselves going about the town shielding her from bigger boys with bigger fists by saying, "Don't punch her. She's not right in the head and doesn't know how to fight." At night they found themselves making sure she had a cover, even if it meant they had to go without. And especially at mealtimes, she was always handed her food first before the rest had a free-for-all. In fact, their cheeks no longer hurt when the muscles bunched up under their eyes and they even forgot to clench their fists to make the smiles stop.

Different people in the town came to the unhappy and embarrassed mother and father and offered to bring about the correct actions, looks, and words in the unnamed girl. They required, of course, bags full of money, and their offers to help sounded like this:

"You are a bunch of low-down scum and your sons are like stunted trees. I can't stand the sight nor sound of your family but send over your stupid, ugly, clumsy daughter and we will knock some sense into her. Don't even think about not paying in full, in advance!"

So time and time again, the girl was sent to be reformed. Time and time again, the ones who tried failed. There were as many methods among them as there were people who tried.

One red-faced woman beat her with a stick and shouted the vilest names at her all day long. But the girl was quickly sent back home when the red-faced woman felt that strange pain in her face. Another person decided that the best training was work, so he worked the girl all day long, making her carry water from a well to his field of thorns. He sent the girl back as quickly as he could because, as he watched her work, he felt that sensation in his cheeks followed by a strange sound coming from his throat, and he thought he would choke. It had a rippling sound and it got in the way of his curses. Though not impossible, even today people find it hard to laugh and curse at the same time.

Now the person who thought he had the best method had a school of girls whom he trained in the finer arts of wickedness and selfishness, fighting and cursing. His claim to success was that people would perform only if there was a reward. The unnamed girl was sent to his training school. There she suffered at the hands of the teacher and the pupils as they tried to entice her with trophies and ribbons to be won if only she would learn to fling her fists, spit out vulgarities, and show bad manners at the table. She disappointed everyone and caused them the same discomfort as she had all the previous people.

In desperation, the parents decided to marry her off and get the problem onto someone else's shoulders. For a high price, they found a man who was willing to take on such a burden. On the wedding day, all the guests had the most awful time with their faces, and no one stayed around afterwards to fight because they had a strange feeling of lightness in their chests and they thought it was heart trouble. They all went home early.

The man decided to call the girl "Bless Me," for in that wicked time those words meant the opposite of what they mean now, and the husband, who had just been paid handsomely to accept this burden, was trying to insult his new wife. He also determined from the start that he was not going to be embarrassed by her deficient ways; rather, he was going to succeed where others had failed. He started out by loading her down with all the bags to carry and made her walk behind him on the way to his house. When they reached the house, he made her immediately get to work cleaning and cooking, and then mending and sewing. What a disappointment he received when she did not throw a pot at his head, or chase him with the broom, or stick him with her pins. She was less right in the head than he could have imagined.

Over a period of time while he did his best to maintain his wealth of wickedness and selfishness, he also experienced the same phenomenal change to his face and to his throat. He tried not to look at Bless Me, but her sudden merry laugh would cause him to look, and he would find himself unable to keep his eyes narrowed and his fists clenched. It fairly wore him down day by day to always be thrown off his guard, and his only comfort was that he had been paid dearly. To hide his embarrassment, he didn't go out as much as he used to, and he never took Bless Me out. However, when people walked past their house, they could hear him saying:

> "Bless Me, quit that awful singing. It hurts my ears!" or

> "Bless Me, this food is slop and you're a slob. Cook me some new food."

The people were sure that eventually the husband would knock the happiness out of Bless Me and make her into a proper angry, selfish, foul-mouthed woman.

But then rumors began to surface that the normal vile words were absent and that not one, but two voices were heard singing. The worst rumor — one that caused everyone to shudder — was that the voice of the husband had said:

"Well, Bless Me, if that wasn't a good meal! I'll clean up the dishes."

After that, people were reluctant to walk close to the house at all, but treated it as if it bore some contagious disease.

In time, Bless Me and her husband gave birth to some children, and each one of them was just like Bless Me. No one had to teach them to be happy and kind and unselfish. They were born that way. And no one tried to make them into proper children by teaching them to punch and curse and take other's toys.

All the people said, "It figures that a mother like Bless Me would have offspring just like herself," and they pitied the poor husband who they supposed was always experiencing pains in his face and ripples from his throat and that awful light feeling in his chest.

Bless Me's children grew up in much the same way that she had, and they were married off with great outlays of money. Eventually, just as the people in that day feared, the number of Bless Me's descendants began to cause a considerable decline in the amount of wickedness and selfishness and hot tempers and flying fists, but not nearly so much that those "virtues" have been wiped out. They can still be found, and they still earn some people respect. But since the world has had the benefit of fairies for so long, beginning with Bless Me and continuing through her family tree, wickedness is not what it used to be a long time ago.

By the way, since no worse fate could be imagined, the people of that day never tired of saying that Bless Me and her unfortunate husband lived happily ever after.

♪

Soup du Jour

Love transforms evil into a pearl.

The roughest shell that you can find is one the Oyster makes: it's gray and coarse like jagged rock, which makes it hard to break. Now, Oysters love their rugged case and like to act real tough, and, inside, all their slimy guts bespeak that they hate fluff. So what a curse it is for them to have to make that thing which in our tongue is called a "pearl" and dangles from earrings.

The curse was started long ago when Oyster was a knave, and was, back then, the meanest cuss to live beneath the waves. Those were the days when Mermaids swam more freely in the seas, and Neptune with his three-pronged spear held all authority. While Oyster feared great Neptune's spear and stayed far from his reach, he drew near Mermaids with disdain as they played on the reefs. Their beauty and agility did drive the Oyster mad: he spawned a plan to clip their fins and turn them all to hags. A Mermaid's fin once it is snipped does make her soon grow old; and, knowing this, the Oyster bit ninety percent, all told.

He worked his woe so secretly while they were fast asleep hugging the coral on the reefs; he snipped them with no peep. But as he neared the last Mermaids, they spied his look of crime and cried out cries ne'er cried before — Ol' Neptune came in time.

King Neptune thrust his mighty spear straight in the Oyster's mouth. But with control, King Neptune stopped and flipped the shell about, "You beauty-hating Oyster fiend, my judgment now I say: one grain of sand I plant in you so you shall ever pay, yes, you shall ever pay!"

See, beauty to a fiend's a curse, thus pearls are born that way. As for the Oyster, when pearl is gone, he's just the Soup of the Day.

THE PUB BY THE DOCK

Evil seeks to control good. Love is beyond control.

Down by the dock is a pub with a reputation that extends all through the world of sailing men. Of course, landlubbers wouldn't understand the affinity sailors have for this pub. To the uninitiated, it looks just like any other joint along the quay.

Only those who have lived on the sea and who have given up the landlocked life can find pleasure in falling into the embrace of the Oyster Chowder Saloon. The strangeness of its name enhances the mystique with which sailors speak about it, and those who have yet to visit the pub listen in awe as warm images float through their minds.

The Oyster Chowder Saloon was given its name by its founder. She called it a saloon because she claimed sailors were the first cowboys — riding the waves instead of the broncos. Though it sat in the vicinity of other pubs, it was very different, from its name to its menu to its decor, because the founder did things her own way and didn't blanch at taking a risk. Everyone she knew told her those were fundamental business errors, and besides, they advised, if you want to attract the men of the sea, your name should conjure up more manly images such as The Rusty Anchor, or The Crusty Barnacle, but not some "kitcheny" image.

Roxanne was the founder. She hadn't meant to found a pub, but when her husband just months before he planned to retire met a tragic death while rounding Cape Horn, one thing led to another. All of his shipmates came to offer their condolences. While they visited Roxanne's little seaside house from where she had sent off and received her husband during the course of so many decades, she set before them bowls of delicious oyster chowder — her husband's favorite. Serving them the chowder alleviated her own grief and acted as a balm to their own souls in the loss of their mate. While they supped, they recalled all the original ways and sayings of Roxanne's husband and were each reluctant to leave as night pressed on to morning. Now they understood why no other port ever interested him but this one.

It started with only these sailing comrades who would visit her when they were in port. She would always give them a grandmotherly welcome, put before them a bowl of oyster chowder, and listen in rapt attention to their stories of the sea. There was no need to stretch a yarn for Roxanne because she knew the sea and any amount of bravery earned approval from her. When one described the height of a wave while clinging only to a halyard, he automatically left out the exaggeration he would've supplied for someone less interested. Roxanne had the kindest words and puff-out-your-chest compliments for the normal everyday courage a sailor had to possess. She could speak poetically about the largeness and deepness of the sea, its kindness and cruelty, and then paint a picture in words of the tiny, intrepid, sailing vessel challenging the strength of the sea with its sheets of cloth on shivers of wood and its mighty men who feared nothing but fear.

Word spread quickly about the effect of Roxanne's ministrations to the sailing man's soul. More and more sailors who put into port would look for Roxanne's seaside house to be fed on oyster chowder as well as on Roxanne's admiration of mariners and tales of the sea.

Roxanne's grown children cautioned her against the intrusion of these strangers. Her children had neither followed the call of the sea as their father had nor possessed an affinity for salty seafaring men. So it was that they convinced their mother to convert her kitchen ministry into a wharfside industry. They feared that some rogue would come along and ruin the trustfulness their mother had for all sailors. They knew that the sea made some men so rough that not even oyster chowder could smooth their sharp edges. Opening a proper pub would limit her risks, they reasoned.

That's the story of why Roxanne bought a little corner of a building right on the wharf and hung up a sign with the name that all the sailors would be looking for. For quite a while the whole setup worked like Roxanne's kitchen, only larger. The same oyster chowder was served and the same Roxanne listened to the sailors wax lyrical about the sea, and she always praised their courage. But as one can guess, the same person who can admire the brave feats of a sailor and serve them oyster chowder with her own hands is not the same person who can make the books balance.

When Roxanne's children convinced her to start the business, she had no money to do it, so a dozen of her children's friends invested their money to help her get started. While Roxanne was serving as matron and ladling out the chowder, there were plenty who were looking for a return on their investment.

One blowing afternoon, one of the main investors slipped in unnoticed and sat in a corner as Roxanne served up chowder and handed around hot beverages. His calculating eye noticed that she didn't always collect the right amount of money from every customer. And then she told a particularly swarthy looking one that his drink was on the house. The investor, of course, had no way to know that this had been the bosom buddy of her late husband, so he went away to report that Roxanne not only lost track of the tabs, but that she also was easily intimidated by the rough sailors, afraid to ask them to pay.

The investors were understandably alarmed. Without consulting Roxanne, they promptly found a bookkeeper and installed him in the backroom. Roxanne found him there the next day. She was glad enough to give over the accounting, the ordering of supplies, and the paying of the bills. For a very short time she was even proud that her humble establishment could boast its very own bookkeeper.

However, all the wind went out of her sails on the day that the bookkeeper tersely informed her that prices would have to be raised and no drinks could be served on the house, and especially, that each sailor had to pay for the chowder by the bowl. Her trademark bottomless soup bowl had to go. It was a becalmed Roxanne who tended the customers and the conversation that day. Some of the sailors wondered if she was sick and others wondered if they had offended.

But it was only for one day that she was in this mood. Wasn't she the heart and soul behind this endeavor! Wasn't she the sole reason that these seafarers looked for her signboard when there were plenty of others to choose from! Didn't her oyster chowder hark back to the days of her own dear husband who would have scoffed at the twiggy sea legs of the trepid bookkeeper! With these and other thoughts, she puffed at her sails and recovered her bearing.

The next day it was the bookkeeper who was told how things were going to be and he was limited to adding up his numbers, ordering supplies, and paying bills. She gave free drinks to whom she willed and filled up the bowls of chowder as often as she pleased. Her poetical discourse on that particular day was strong enough to rouse the sleeping poets inside of the sailors. But a blow was coming that she could not predict.

Sneaking out while she was holding forth and fulfilling her vision of the Oyster Chowder Saloon, the bookkeeper raised the alarm among the investors. At the end of the day, Roxanne found herself facing the whole group of them. She was ill prepared to stand up to the education they all possessed, not to mention the legitimate claim they had on her business. Without any stirrings in their hearts for what she meant to the sailors, they declared the

Oyster Chowder Saloon off-limits to her. In an orderly fashion, they read off her crimes against good business and declared her an albatross around the neck of the pub. They promised to re-evaluate in a few months. If the Oyster Chowder Saloon was turning a profit, they would consider allowing her back — if she would follow the rules.

Her children tried to console her. Her friends said they had known it wouldn't work. Roxanne sat in her empty kitchen alone. Her grief returned and she felt very much a widow.

In true good business fashion, the investors hired a no-nonsense manager. The new face seemed anathema to the regulars and they quit coming. The first-timers, assuming they had found the Oyster Chowder Saloon, wondered why the images in their head didn't match what they had found.

It didn't take long for its reputation to change and become just like that of any other pub. In fact, the new manager wanted to change its name as soon as possible. The oyster chowder continued to be served, but without its balm, and there was no one to hold forth on the mystery of the sea and the bravery of the men who rode the waves. The new manager refused to part with any encouraging words, and the sailors got the impression that he used to be a galley cook, for that's how he passed out the drinks and slopped out the chowder. Tablecloths were put in storage and curtains were replaced with shutters. Eventually, the chowder pot was not even filled up. Business diminished as the signs of Roxanne disappeared.

Roxanne hoped that she would be called back to attract the former level of clientele. It never happened. Her heart felt a pang every time she saw her signboard blowing in the wind. It meant to her the memory of her husband, the magic of her oyster chowder, her own way of empathizing with the sailors, and the way the home atmosphere was such an attraction to the ones who spent their lives on the open and dangerous sea.

And then Roxanne gave it up, and she was happy once again. She cooked up her oyster chowder and let it be known among her husband's old cronies that her kitchen was again open for "business." From that day onward, her kitchen table was always crowded and she carried on life in her way, risky or not.

The last that was seen of the Oyster Chowder Saloon was when the sign was taken down. The business had gone under and was bought out by another pub. A passing sailor saw the discarded signboard in the alley behind the pub and he picked it up. It now hangs in the seaward window of Roxanne's kitchen where all the drinks are on the house and all the chowder bowls are bottomless.

♪

Helios, Move Over!

Evil demands sovereignty. Love is humble.

"Limits? Limits? What are limits? The only limit is yourself! You are sovereign in your own life, with or without lots of wealth." With these words the Millionairess mounted platform of her craft. When they asked her if she felt fear, her reply was just a laugh.

As the countdown for her journey was broadcast throughout the land, commentators all did marvel as she raised her steady hand; her last word before the blastoff was her motto said again. "Limits only live in your mind — take the future in your hand!"

At her funeral three days later, commentators speculated that some faulty engineering was the tragic cause of death. Limits! Limits! There are limits, heaven-sent or from below; when you think there are no limits, watch out for a mortal blow.

☙

EARTH - MOON TALK

Evil fails to consider others. Love is considerate.

"Are you truly my friend?"

"You know I am. Don't I always stick right by you?"

"Yeah. Didn't mean to doubt you, but sometimes I see a reflection of the Big Guy in you and I begin to think, well, you know, that maybe you're just hanging around me because he told you to."

"No way. I'm only here because I want to be here."

"Good. I had to be sure because I'm making a plan."

"Oh, no. Why does that make me feel nervous? Is it just another spaceship plan?"

"No! It's way bigger than that. But it's only fair to warn you, since you have stuck by me, that it might upset your ways a little."

"You're not building a bridge over to me, are you?"

"Are you crazy? No working relationship could stand that kind of strain. I'm just changing course, that's all."

"Whoa, it's a good thing you're telling me. What are you going to do, go backwards or something?"

"Now, look. The way I see it, the Big Guy, he has all of us where he wants us. Some of us he wants real near, and those get most of his attention. Some of us he lets have a pretty long rein, and my guess is, those guys don't want to be noticed or they would've already come in closer — like I'm planning to do."

"Now, wait a minute. I'm just a little cog in the wheel and maybe I don't see what's wrong with your position, but do you really think you can do that and survive?"

"Why not? Venus is doing okay for herself. And Mercury literally basks in the Big Guy's praise. No wonder he's fast. But what am I? I'm neither one of the favorites nor one of the trusty independent ones."

"Do you really think you would want to be in Mercury's place or way out on the fringe?

"I guess I just want a change. I want to do something that gets me recognition. Why can't I move in a little closer? I would look good with a bit more tan, and I'd like to see what I could accomplish with a shorter year. Who knows, maybe I could even compete with Venus for the Big Guy's attention."

"Have you asked him about this? I mean, does he have any idea you're thinking of jumping out of your track and moving in because you want more of his notice?"

"Look, I asked him once, okay. He hardly gave me the time of day. He just reeled off all this mumbo-jumbo about my being where I need to be, and how my conditions are more perfect than anyone else's, and, like … how would he know? He hasn't been where I am. He just wanted to shut me up."

"Well, you know, there is a balance to things in a big organization like this, and it is his job to sort of keep an eye on things."

"You really are his spy, aren't you? I thought you said you were with me."

"I am with you, but I've got to think of myself, too."

"Oh, so you think another planet would be safer to be around than I am? By the way, I didn't see you the other night. Were you off hunting down some other position for yourself?"

"Really, now you're getting paranoid. You know that every month I go off, I mean, I turn my light off. Boy, let me tell you, you'd know it if I left you even for a second. I think you take me for granted."

"Yeah, sorry. I didn't mean to forget about that once-a-month thing where you have to switch off, and I know, without a doubt, that only you can keep my oceans organized. I'd be swamped without you. When I make a move, I definitely want to take you with me. It's just that, well, sometimes a moon has a way of looking that just keeps us guys a little unsure. Like sometimes, it seems you're only half with me, and then at other times, you seem to workday and night. I guess I'm just feeling a bit shaky about trying to break out of my rut, and it makes me a little suspicious."

"How in the world could you be suspicious of me? I've stuck with you through all your major successes and failures. It hasn't mattered to me when some of those other guys make the news and their moons are photographed and given exotic names. I had my day once when everyone was interested in me, but I prefer just doing my own job and not attracting much attention."

"Well, uh, I was hoping you'd be up for some more media attention. I mean, if I jump my tracks and move in closer, it'll make a splash. I don't think it's been done before, you know, without a bona fide promotion or at least a nod from the Big Guy. And if I can pull it off, there'd be a lot of interest in me and perhaps in the moon who stuck by me."

"Oh, please, don't misunderstand me and think that I'm trying to represent the Big Guy when I say this, but my job means a lot to me. When you jump your tracks and make your bold move to get noticed and grab some of the benefits of being closer in, don't you think it might backfire? I mean, we might both find ourselves out of a position. The Big Guy might just decide that if you don't like your track around him, you can just go find yourself another system."

"That's just it. I've always wanted to test out just how much importance he places on my position. And there's only one way to find out. Since he's so preoccupied with just keeping everything on course, I have to do something risky. If the Big Guy's as hot as he thinks he is, he'll recognize that I'm valuable spinning a little closer to him. Who knows what could be accomplished if I was just closer in?"

"Well, I'll try to keep things in order when you do make your jump, and I hope being closer in won't show up my weaknesses. But ... do you think you should consult any others before you take this leap?"

"Nah. They'll hang on."

♪

The Last Cent

Evil knows how to twist a vow.
Love unties twisted knots.

The day before his mother died she slipped into his tiny palm a coin she'd had since she was young, and then she said, "My son, be calm. Remember, as you keep this coin, that if you never let it go, you'll never die without a cent, no matter which way fate does blow." He made the vow.

The years went by, he's now a man with fortune made in silken trade. He even owns a fleet of ships and has a mansion made of jade.

But one gray day a fell wind blew and sunk his fleet and brought him ruin. He sold his mansion at a loss and all his wealth was from him hewn. Then in the dark a mem'ry came of some old coin he'd hid away. He searched and found it in a bag — on open palm he watched it lay. Remembering what his mother said, he closed his hand and sat to sleep. He was forgotten by his friends; his final home is now the street.

'Twas on a chill morn that they found his lifeless form with fist shut tight. The next day's papers 'cross the world reported who had died that night:

A homeless man died millionaire! He did not have a single heir to pass the proceeds of the sale of priceless coin his fist did bear.

A collector paid a royal mint for that old coin his mother gave, which he was bound to keep unspent to honor her unto his grave. There is a part of all of us we will not part with for the world; but if that part is spent at last, it can combat what fate does hurl.

The Street Sweeper

Evil can be inflicted on the innocent.
Love covers a multitude of sins.

Not very long ago there was a man who inspired fear in the most stalwart of hearts. He didn't go by his given name but by his crime name, Mr. Broom. This was an acquired name because it aptly described the way that he cleaned people out of their money, their dignity, and sometimes their lives.

Like a large sweeping broom, he could rob both the wealthy, who had excess, and the destitute, who had only a few coins. His worst crime was to rob mothers and fathers of their sons by enticing the boys away with promises of money and power. Once he had the boys, he robbed them of their dignity by making them into his slaves. To keep their lives, they had to follow his orders by bringing increase to his own store of money and power. Not a few of those boys were robbed of their very lives when they crossed Mr. Broom. With a few strokes they were gone.

Mr. Broom had long ago swept his own conscience free of any remorse or regret. He felt nothing but satisfaction as he became more powerful and more people groveled at his feet for his approval. So thoroughly had his conscience been wiped free of knowing right from wrong that he could make wicked schemes for others to carry out and receive the punishment for, while he looked on innocently and smiled. Mr. Broom was as ingenious about looking out for his own survival as he was avid about destroying others.

The city where Mr. Broom operated hated him, but not openly, because to hate him openly was to invite him to come in with his clever schemes and brush out a life or a business. Besides, so many people in the city had chosen to cower before him that his survival was guaranteed. No one could speak a word against Mr. Broom without it getting back to him, and any who dared withhold their sons from him paid for it over and over again.

The city leaders were helpless against the power of Mr. Broom. If they tried to be clever to curb his crime, he was cleverer and punished them for trying. If they tried to capture Mr. Broom in the act of robbing or stealing, he escaped the net and let others get caught. By keeping his life, he was destroying all that was good in the city. Some even joked (out the side of their mouths) that he should be made mayor and thereby redefine crime as "business as usual."

At the pinnacle of his success, he moved in complete freedom and felt rewarded for his cleanly-swept conscience. Just as he was congratulating himself on being the most feared, the most powerful, and the most unconquerable, a young boy was brought to him to be made into his next slave. The boy was brought before him to be taught who Mr. Broom was by making him crawl on his knees and beg for Mr. Broom's favor.

There was wicked laughter all around when the boy refused to fall down on his knees, and the laughter swelled to a crescendo as some of Mr. Broom's henchmen beat the boy from behind to make him fall. Just as the second blow fell upon his back and while Mr. Broom was enjoying the show, the boy looked up and his face changed. At the change, Mr. Broom's face changed as well. He stared with his mouth agape. He seemed paralyzed as the boy approached him and whispered something into his ear. As soon as the boy was done speaking, he vanished into thin air. Mr. Broom got up and walked away as one who sees and hears nothing around him.

†

Sometime later in the streets of the city, a street sweeper appeared. Though no one knew where he came from, no one bothered to ask. The street sweeper was out early every morning with his long-handled broom. The sound of him pushing the rubbish along the street became as dependable as the songs of the morning birds. The whoosh, whoosh of the broom went up and down the streets while the people were in their last moments of sleep, and for many it became the signal that morning had come.

The streets of the city had not been swept regularly until the street sweeper arrived. Before his appearance, the residents and the shopkeepers tried to keep their own sidewalks cleared of debris, but they usually just pushed it out into the street. Now that the street sweeper was a fixture in the city, the streets were free of trash. Whatever was pushed off the sidewalks, he collected with his long-handled broom.

For a long time the street sweeper worked and no one ever spoke to him, but one morning a boy was waiting on the curb when the street sweeper came past. He was searching in vain for something. "I lost my favorite marble on the street and I can't find it." The street sweeper paused in his motion and with his own hands sorted through the sweepings at the end of his long-handled broom. A thorough search turned up the favored marble. The look on the young boy's face as he admired the marble and offered his sincere thanks warmed the street sweeper's heart.

From that day onward he kept a lookout for toys that might have been lost, and he dropped them into a bag slung over his back. It became known that if you lost something in the street, the street sweeper would find it and keep it in his bag until you met him and asked for it. Sometimes a missing treasure did not look like anything special, but whenever any child asked him to look for something, the sweeper stopped his motion and sorted through the sweepings with his own hands until it was found. In this way the street sweeper came to recognize all the treasures of children.

Each time the street sweeper returned something to a child from the bag on his back or found it just at the moment the child asked for it, his heart was warmed all over again. Because it felt so good, he looked for other things which might have been lost on the street and he watched for the people who were missing them. On many occasions he returned the one missing earring, a dropped wallet, a treasured photo, and other small things which are dropped onto a street and are hard to find but sorely missed.

Many people assumed that the street sweeper couldn't speak because he never did. He communicated only with actions and gestures. Sometimes people were unkind to the street sweeper if his broom happened to offend them. He was, after all, a common laborer, and he was supposed to look out for others and wait for them to have the right of way. No matter what thoughtless thing was said or how roughly his long-handled broom was kicked, the street sweeper never lifted his hand or opened his mouth to protest. No matter how they taunted or how they insulted the street sweeper, he never took up the challenge but went right on pushing his broom and collecting the litter in front of it.

Meanwhile, in the absence of Mr. Broom from the city, crime fell sharply and parents managed to hang on to their sons and more people kept their lives. Goodness seemed to be sprouting up everywhere, and to top it all off, the streets were even clean. Years and years went by. Everything was so different than it was in the days of Mr. Broom, that when parents told their young children the awful stories, the children could not imagine it.

It happened one day as the street sweeper was pushing his broom along Main Street that he saw a scrap of paper leave the possession of a hurried man dressed in a suit. Having learned the importance that such small scraps of paper can carry, the street sweeper rescued the fleeing note. The man had discovered his loss and was frantically searching the ground when the street sweeper presented him with it.

At first glance, the man mistrusted the offering, but then quickly snatched at the scrap, crumpling it into his hand, saying, "It's worthless. You didn't read it, did you?" He continued, "because if you did, I'll have you fire ..." but then suddenly stopped, changing both his tone and his idea.

"Oh, you're the guy who sweeps the streets day in and day out without any pay. You are just the guy I'm looking for."

The two stood for a long time together — the street sweeper leaning upon his broom handle and the man in the suit speaking hurriedly and with passion. What the street sweeper heard gave him much to think about, though the man in the suit only gave him until midnight to come to a decision. The man in the suit would be waiting for him in the French restaurant at the bay — on the north side of town.

The proposition to the street sweeper had been staggering, and perhaps the reward of his humble service. The man in the suit was concerned about the office of mayor, which was at the moment filled by a "stubborn" individual who had "lost touch with the common people." He was looking for the perfect candidate who could challenge the mayor. Someone from the working class might just be the ticket. He needed someone who would evoke deep feelings among the people of the city, and when the note had been handed back to him, it all came together. The street sweeper was admired and appreciated by all, and the man in the suit would be his campaign manager, coach, and counsel — there to help him know how to wield power for "everyone's benefit."

On the north side of town, a newspaper reporter was disembarking from a train and about to head for the French restaurant. A close associate of his had hinted that a big story would break there around midnight, and he could have it. The only hint was that it involved the mayoral race and the familiar but humble street sweeper.

The reporter was just coming off the train when he saw the street sweeper getting onto the southbound train. He had looked at the platform clock to check the time, afraid that he had already missed the promised scoop. It was fifteen until midnight and the street sweeper was going the wrong way.

The reporter instinctively felt the big story was not at the restaurant but was, instead, getting back onto the train. He sprinted and boarded the southbound train just before it pulled out.

The street sweeper was sitting alone, except for his long-handled broom propped against the aisle seat beside him. After a time, during which the street sweeper only looked out the window at the city lights, another man entered the train car which was only occupied by the street sweeper, his broom, and the reporter.

The reporter quietly took out his note pad and pencil and began to make notes. The newcomer was the exact replica of the street sweeper — minus the broom. It was his twin. The reporter was at a loss to make a notation that accurately described the shudder which went through him. In fact, he was stunned into watchful silence.

The twin of the street sweeper sat down behind the seat that held the broom while the street sweeper continued to gaze out the window. The twin's voice was low, but the reporter strained all his senses to catch his words and record what was said:

"I'm surprised to find you going south. When I saw you so close to the north side, I gave up hope of ever seeing you again. I figured the opportunity to be in charge again, and this time to be legitimate, would be too tempting, even if it meant never seeing me again. You could have ruled the city as you once did, and that crafty man in the suit would have found himself, before he knew it, swept right under the carpet. When I came to you that day in the form of a boy, I didn't know if you would take to heart what I said."

The reporter found himself leaning forward as the street sweeper himself began to talk:

"While you were alive I could bear the beatings our father gave us since we shared each other's pain. But on the day he hit you too hard and killed you, something in me died, and I ran away. The last thing I said to our father as he stood over your lifeless body was that I never wanted to be like him. So when you whispered in my ear that day that I had become like our father — only worse — the whole world blacked out in front of me."

The reporter was scribbling madly in his notebook, though he couldn't make much sense of it.

The street sweeper continued, "When you told me what I had to do to reach you rather than end up with our father, all I could do was do it, first out of shock, but then later out of contentment. And when the ultimate test you predicted came, it was tempting, because I could have done well as the mayor. But I studied my broom as I was heading toward the restaurant, and I knew I couldn't do it. So, Brother, I did what you had pleaded for: I did a humble job, gave back instead of taking, never raised my voice against anyone, and finally, when the chance came to get back into a position of power came, well ... I suppose you saw it, didn't you?"

"Yes, Brother, I did."

The reporter was still scratching out these last words, not even believing he was really hearing this conversation, when the street sweeper and his twin got off the train at a deserted station far from the city limits. He had been unaware that the train had even stopped, and now he was stuck on the train while his big scoop got off. He turned in his seat and watched the two. They stood alone on the platform. However, with the reflection of the inside lights upon the window and the dimness of the platform light, the reporter's eyes were tricked to make it appear that the two disappeared.

At the next station he hurriedly changed directions in order to get back to that dimly lit platform. There, leaning against the trash can, was only the long-handled broom. The reporter took it in his hands and examined it. Carved along the handle were these words, *Power reveals corruption since the corrupted desire power.* Though no one ever believed (or published) the reporter's story, that broom leans in the corner of his office to this day.

♪

A Tiny Little Man

Evil exacts respect. Love is merciful.

    He's a tiny little man though he's over six feet tall with a puny little job but he acts like lord of all. When he strides into the room he expects from you respect though to you he will give none as he closely does inspect every tiny little jot of the work that he demands, and if things are not just right then out flies a reprimand.
    Yes, we surely all desire in the rubbish him to toss, but we never have the nerve 'cos that guy is still the boss.

☙

The Signmaker and His Son

Evil's public face is deceptive.
Love is transparent in its goodness.

A signmaker set up shop in a village. Although there were other signmakers in the village, he began to seek customers. He possessed about himself a friendliness and humbleness that enabled him to go throughout the village, newcomer and stranger that he was, stopping in at all the establishments to announce that he was open for business.

Generally, people in that village believed that if you were a tradesman worth your salt, you would have proper documentation of where and with whom you had apprenticed and where and for whom you had plied your trade. It was always best if among your customers you could name royalty or landed gentry. In the absence of these proofs, however, the signmaker put himself forward in person and merely, in a friendly and naïve way, invited the merchants and populace of the village to come to his shop for their signmaking needs. His manner was very disarming, so no one took offense, although it was very strange.

Some, at first, came out of curiosity because this signmaker had been quite unorthodox in establishing his business. They wondered if he used the same methods as the other signmakers, and certainly they wondered if he charged a different price. When the first ones reported how they found the signmaker hard at work, and how he stopped everything to attend to them, and how, before they knew it, they were ordering a new sign for their own shops, and especially, how they themselves were the ones allowed to fix their own prices, others listened in utter amazement.

The business of the signmaker naturally grew with this arrangement. In truth, the signmaker endeared himself to the village populace by his other unorthodox practice of delivering the signs himself and hanging them free of charge, unless one would count the invitation to the backroom for a drink as any kind of payment. Being still a newcomer to the village, the signmaker had no friends to speak of except those who became his clients. When he had a lull in his work, he would pay a visit to any shops where his sign work hung and commence to cement a friendship by purchasing goods from that shop. As was his manner, he always inquired after the health and well-being of the family.

Any suspicions which might have arisen by his arrival and unusual practices were soon diminished by his adoption of the village's customs and dialect and by his humble ambitions. The signmaker refused to take any jobs that naturally belonged to the other signmakers. He would casually ask any new customer if they had ever had a sign made. If they answered yes, he would encourage them to return to the same signmaker they had used before. By insisting that he only wanted to make signs for those who had had no signs before, he carved out a niche for himself in the village that made even the other signmakers not oppose his presence. Also, he specialized in very simple designs. He became known as the one who willingly produced the humble and affordable signs.

The signmaker had a son. It was a thing that people noticed immediately since he was seen going about the village with his small son in tow. However, as the signmaker never drew attention to the son standing in his shadow and the son never drew attention to himself, it was possible to overlook the small boy standing just behind his father. Occasionally, an old woman would notice the boy as he followed the signmaker pace for pace, and she would remark, "Now there goes a future signmaker, and doesn't he look the very image of his father!" At this, a smile would creep onto the son's face, but it would quickly disappear when the signmaker turned a disapproving look toward the old woman's comment.

In the workshop, the boy was always near the signmaker's elbow. He made himself useful from morning till night by holding tools and mixing dyes and sweeping up the floor. It was evident that he admired his signmaker father and had even learned his father's way of being friendly and humble with all the clients. By standing near the signmaker's side, he had learned the trade as easily as he had learned to walk.

The signmaker allowed him to stand behind him and never objected to the way he helped with the tools and the dyes and the sweeping. Yet the signmaker never thought, "Oh, what a boon that my son wants to be like I am. I can teach him all that I know and pass along my business to him." Quite to the contrary, the signmaker thought nothing of the son's future except that he would surely not be a signmaker and take over the business, because a trade is a calling, not an inheritance. As the son grew older and a bit taller, he continued to admire the signmaker and to watch and imitate his ways.

One day the signmaker went out into the village and left a sign he was working on unfinished. The son, staying behind in the shop, noticed the unfinished work and decided to surprise his father. All the time his father was away, the son wielded the tools upon the wood until he had not only carved the basic lettering, but also added some embellishments around it. And then, before his father returned, the son mixed the dyes, stained the signboard, put away the tools, and swept the floor. Then he placed the sign in plain view so that when his father returned, he would see in an instant that he was destined to follow in his footsteps.

When the signmaker returned, he saw his son standing expectantly beside the newly finished sign (which was of far better workmanship than he could do). Without any words of commendation, the signmaker looked off to the side into the tool tray and accused, "You broke a chisel." The son began to say that it had already been broken when the signmaker silenced him with a backhanded slap across the face which completely wiped away his beaming smile and caused him to inadvertently knock the new sign over from where it stood propped. The signmaker reminded the son with curses that they had little enough to live on already without the son breaking valuable tools. When he noticed that the sign had fallen over and split down the middle, he further accused the son of wasting materials.

Thus, the son painfully learned the harsh side of his father. If any had known that the signmaker had this violent side, they would have wagged their heads and said, "We like the signmaker well enough, and he has been a humble and generous friend, but surely this is a flaw that bears looking into." The son, however, adored his father so much that he never allowed the violence to come to light. He suffered blows and curses in silence. Then one day he gave up the idea of ever becoming a signmaker. After that, he no longer wanted to stand by the signmaker's side and hand him the tools and mix the dyes and sweep the floor, but that was just when the signmaker insisted he do so.

The signmaker's shop in time became a prison to the son who was now no longer a child. The son himself knew that the blows and the curses were undeserved and that he never intended any malice to the signmaker by thinking that he could become a signmaker. The blows and curses continued whenever the son dropped a tool or spilled the dye, and once, in retort, the son blurted out that the signmaker really had no skill and that he never really had wanted to be like him. At this, the signmaker knowingly nodded his head and declared that all the blows and curses had therefore been deserved since the son had been lying about wanting to be like him.

Strangely, then, the son did feel himself deserving of the punishment, especially as the signmaker continued to go out among the villagers in his friendly and humble way. The son no longer looked the very image of the signmaker and did not care to stand in his shadow, and especially he did not want to hear what any old lady might say as she passed by.

One day the signmaker announced that he was taking on an apprentice. He had been making his friendly rounds in the village to check on the soundness of the signboards he had hung for his clients who were now his friends when one of them put forward a young boy who felt called to learn a trade. The signmaker pulled the boy to his side and told him that he had been looking a long time for a suitable apprentice, and that someday, perhaps, he could take over the business.

When the signmaker brought the young boy to the shop and the son saw his place beside his father taken over by a stranger, he packed his bag and left by the back door. As the door slammed shut, the signmaker only pulled the young apprentice closer and showed him how to hold the tools.

Naturally, the people in the village inquired after the son whom they no longer saw looking the very image of the father and standing in his shadow. The signmaker casually explained that the son had grown restless and left with nary a word. At this, the people wagged their heads and felt sorry for the signmaker. The signmaker looked humble and friendly and said it was a shame, but how wonderful that he had found an apprentice who really wanted to learn the trade and take over the business someday.

The signmaker allowed the apprentice to stay at his elbow and learn the trade, but the boy possessed neither the skill nor the interest in signmaking that the son had. He kept the tools in disarray and spilled the dyes and left the floor unswept. As the signmaker's business began to decline, he never thought to dismiss or chasten the apprentice because the boy was taken on to cement a friendship he had with a client. He praised the boy to all who would listen.

Meanwhile, the son settled himself in a village far away, and after many years of hard work, established himself as an admired and respected signmaker. Occasionally a customer when admiring a new sign would ask where he had learned his craft. The son always named his father with respect, but invited no further questions. Over the years, he took on many apprentices as well as trained his own son in the trade. When an old woman happened to remark, "Now there goes a future signmaker," the small son allowed a smile to creep onto his face which grew larger as his father returned an approving look toward the old woman's comment.

♪

Hyena's Love

Evil laughter always has a victim. Love's doesn't.

Do hyenas love each other as they scavenge for their food? Do they stand up for a brother? Do they work for common good? Aren't they more the kind of creature that we think of as a beast? Oh, so lowly is their stature — calling carrion a feast!

Do hyenas love each other as they laugh the day away? Or is laughter a dark cover hiding what they really say? In the dark they know each other by the cunning in their eyes: glowing red, they can discover any enemy's disguise. Joining in the task before them, growing strong in unity, they search out another's weakness, chasing him up in a tree.

Looking down we now discover as they laugh beneath the tree, that they do not love each other 'cos their true love's up the tree.

଴ଷ

The Candle on the Shelf

Evil demands to be served. Love serves.

In a large old estate surrounded by a thick forest lived an elderly man whose days of influence were well gone. He lived on among his possessions, but his rooms and halls were empty and lonely. He's not very important to this story except that the affairs of his life had spread out like the roots of an old tree, and everywhere they touched people experienced misery and fear.

One of his shorter roots was wrapped around his housekeeper who was also his cook. The old man had hired her when she was young and inexperienced. Through the course of the years, she had learned to perform her duties always and on time. She so grew into the job of housekeeper that where the job stopped and where she began was indistinguishable. But she is not very important to this story either, except that now she is a cross old woman who orders people around and doesn't tolerate those who don't perform their jobs always and on time. (Once upon a time she had wanted to marry a man who was a gardener for the estate, but the old man of the estate forbade the marriage and fired the gardener. She never protested.)

There was a young girl in the estate. She came to work there not by way of her own choice. And though her parents are not important to this story, they were at the end of another of the old man's roots. When the old man's housekeeper needed a helper, he forgave a portion of the parents' indebtedness for the services of their daughter.

This story is about the young girl, Emily, whose job it was to obey the housekeeper, which she must do always and on time. She did whatever the housekeeper asked and she never lifted her voice to complain when the work was too heavy or too mundane. Many times she was glad that her mother had taught her to keep house with imagination and creativity. When she was performing her tasks, she imagined that she was doing them with her mother instead of the mean housekeeper, and very often she entertained herself with made-up stories while she peeled potatoes or scrubbed the stone floor.

It angered the housekeeper, however, that Emily went about her work without a complaint. The housekeeper gave her every demeaning and degrading task there was to do, and sometimes upon finding it done without a flaw, assigned her to do it again.

Now, there was one task which made Emily quail and it did not escape the notice of the housekeeper, who you can be sure was glad (in her wicked heart) to discover it. This task made all the skin turn to goose flesh on the young girl. It made her knees feel week. It especially caused her heart to pound and her breath to come in gasps. But that is why the housekeeper decided to use the candle on the shelf to finally break the young girl's pleasant, willing spirit.

One day the housekeeper told the girl to go to the cellar and bring up apples, potatoes, and a melon. She handed the girl the half-burnt candle that stood in a wooden candleholder on the shelf. The black hole of the cellar seemed too large a darkness for a little half-burnt candle, but the housekeeper demanded it, so Emily descended the steep stone steps. The cool, dank air caused the candle flame to sway and bend. Her feet scraped the hard dirt floor. She held the candle higher to shed more light around the cellar.

The clay jars lined up on shelves all around the cellar cast great shadowy shapes behind them. The smell of rotting fruit assaulted her nostrils. The floor crunched under her feet, and she heard movement beyond the small circle of light that the candle gave off. Cautiously, she walked to the wall and put her hand into the potato bin. The first one she touched scurried away. A shiver shook her whole frame. She could not hold the candle and pick out potatoes at the same time, so she put the candle on the ground to fill her bag. An awful darkness rose up behind her. Something dropped from the low ceiling into her hair. Cringing, she hastened her picking from the potato and apple bins and then hunted in the dark for the melons. She found them under the wooden shelving, covered with spider webs. The first one she reached for was merely a shell with a dead mouse inside. With a pounding heart and shaking limbs, she chose another and quickly scrambled up the stairs. Stumbling into the light at the top, Emily handed her bag to the housekeeper, and the housekeeper, with satisfaction, noted her shortness of breath and her pale face.

The next day, as Emily was serenely polishing the silverware and laying each spoon and fork down as if they were children being put gently to bed, the housekeeper took pleasure in interrupting her, demanding more fruit and vegetables to be brought up from below at once. At the mention of the cellar, Emily's face fell. The candle was taken off the shelf and thrust into her hands. This time the housekeeper wanted fruit and vegetables with neither bruise nor blemish, which would require the girl to stay longer in the creeping and crawling cellar.

The next day, the housekeeper was again pleased to interrupt the girl, this time as she was dusting the banisters, pretending that each baluster was a tall soldier guarding a castle. The candle was taken from the shelf. Emily gripped it trustingly as if it were a hand to hold in the dark. The housekeeper waited until she had reached the dirt floor and then shut the door and slid the bolt in place. Having completed the task, Emily knocked on the door to be let up. The housekeeper walked slowly to the door and slid the bolt back with leisure. She found delight in the traces of tears on Emily's cheeks.

This went on day after day until more food than was needed had been brought up from the cellar. Emily understood how the housekeeper was tormenting her, but she dared not raise her voice for fear of what worse thing could happen to her, or even yet to her parents.

Finally, the day came when Emily had no imaginary stories or any other tender thoughts keeping her company. She was now just going through the motions, dreading the summons that was soon to come. The housekeeper reveled in seeing Emily's spirit sputtering out. With a stony smile, she recited to Emily yet another long selection of fruit and vegetables to find. She thrust at her a cumbersome bag in which to load them.

The candle from the shelf was lit, but by this time, the wax formed only a mere pool around the wick. The housekeeper and Emily both knew that it would not last even until the bottom of the stairs. At this, Emily spoke and asked for a new candle, to which the housekeeper replied that there were no others to replace the one on the shelf. Still, the housekeeper insisted that the food had to be brought up — always and on time.

It was just as Emily had feared. The flame flickered out at the bottom of the stairs and she was left in thick and utter darkness. The housekeeper had shut and bolted the door already. Emily gave a shudder as the sounds and the dank air surrounded her with invisible creeping fingertips, and a cry convulsed from her innocent and frightened frame. All the cruel ploys of the housekeeper came together in that wretched moment and she began to quiver. Her body shook and her tears coursed down her cheeks. They fell onto the extinguished candle.

Almost imperceptibly the candle began to glow, and then the glow floated up and spread itself out in front of the girl's wondering eyes. Her cheeks were wet and her breath was coming in short gasps, but the glow that lifted off the candle and sparkled in front of her didn't arouse fear. In the center of the glow was a tiny fairy whose gown looked like a candle flame, and the light from the fairy was more than the light of a dozen candles.

The fairy simply and quietly (knowing the housekeeper was listening at the door) told the girl that her tears had called her out of the candle. "This is a magic candle, my child, and when innocent tears fall upon it, I am released to spread out my flame and give light to calm all shattered nerves and tormented thoughts. Now, take your bag and go about your gathering. I will go in front of you with my light."

With the fairy's bright light, Emily filled up her bag and stayed in the cellar long enough for all her tears to dry and for her breath to become even and soft again. When Emily knocked on the door to ask the wicked housekeeper to let her out, the fairy slipped back into the remnant of the candle.

At length, Emily came up into the light of the kitchen. The housekeeper examined her closely. Her brow grew dark when she could not find the marks of tears or a hint of a pale face. The housekeeper glowered at the girl and demanded to see the quality of what she had brought in her bag. When it was all shown to be without bruises or gashes, the housekeeper's face grew red. As Emily turned to her next task with a pleasant face and a content look in her eye, the housekeeper took a deep breath and rushed at her, her face contorted and arms outstretched. Just then, a pain from inside the housekeeper's body seized her and caused her to crumple to the ground.

No one was ever to know of the housekeeper's dark cruelty toward Emily, for Emily never repeated it. After the housekeeper died, no new housekeeper was hired because the old man of the estate died soon afterward. Before Emily returned to her waiting family, she took down the candle from the shelf one last time. Scraping at a tiny fleck of black — all that was left of the wick — she gently lifted it, lit it, and from its brief flame, ignited a tall new candle, allowing it to burn only a moment. Then she placed the new candle in the holder and left it on the shelf just in case there should come another who might need it.

♪

THE FALLING TREE

Love embraces evil's victims.

Does the lonely falling tree when no one's there to hear make no sound but silently hush against the ground?

Do forgotten fallen brave when war has come and gone cease to cry and silently lie still where they died?

Does the young and helpless one whom some cruel fate now slays have no choice since silently she cries without a voice?

All the lonely falling trees in heaven do make sound. ... Pausing now, so silently, I hear them hit the ground.

A Note in the Bottle

Evil uses the naïve & kindhearted. Love endures.

The orphanage sat on the edge of town. It had a bad reputation to match its old crumbling building. Miss Crow was the superintendent. The orphans, for all their other lacks, never lacked in laughter from making jokes about how similar she was to the feathered beast of the same name. They even called the orphanage 'The Nest,' but only when Miss Crow was out of earshot because she insisted that they daily offer up thanks for the roof over their heads, the food in their bellies, and the clothes on their scrawny backs.

There was one girl, Brenda, who was not an orphan but who also partook in the secret laughter about Miss Crow's voice, spindly bird legs, and beak-like nose. She was the orphanage's cleaning girl, and although she wasn't orphaned, she was as good as. Her parents had turned her out to work and had made Miss Crow her legal guardian. She did her work alone and she laughed alone since the orphans suspected that she was in league with the superintendent, and so they kept her out of their most delicious communing. At times, she wished she were truly orphaned just so she could have friends. Miss Crow treated her like a poor undeserving orphan, and the orphans treated her like a trespassing crow. And belonging nowhere increased Brenda's misery.

†

Peter lived in a bright clean house. His mother still looked after him even though he earned his own living by delivering milk. Every morning he put on his clean jacket and trousers, donned the company hat that he was so proud of, drank down the cup of hot tea his mother had steeped for him, and kissed her goodbye. His pedal-powered three-wheeled delivery wagon was kept dry and clean underneath the awning of their little house. Just before he pedaled off to the dairy to get his load of milk bottles, he tested the bell and admired its shine, straightened his hat to just the right angle using the bell as a mirror, and gave a salute, for he liked to think of himself as a soldier in the war against rickets. Delivering milk to all the houses of the town, whether the grandest estate or the lowliest hovel, was a service requiring the utmost in discipline, dedication, and determination. In fact, Peter repeated these words over and over to himself as he pedaled up and down the hills of his town and especially when he made his final delivery to the edge of town.

The orphanage ordered one bottle of milk per orphan per day. To Peter it was a major military maneuver to set down four crates of full bottles and pick up four crates of empty bottles. Each time he set the empty bottles inside his wooden wagon, he considered that rickets had received a mighty setback, and it was all because of his willingness to serve under the motto of Discipline, Dedication, and Determination.

The orphanage also reinforced his own love of his clean bright home and his mother. Peter knew that with only one parent living, he had just barely escaped being an orphan himself. Many were the nights as a young boy that he was glad to hear his mother snoring in her room because it reminded him that he wasn't an orphan.

Usually something about the orphanage would often start an adventure in his head. It might have been a child's cry or a sharp rebuke or an unclean smell or perhaps the barrenness of the garden. On his return to the dairy with all the empty bottles jangling in his cart, his story would unfold with him, in military sharpness, rescuing any number of mistreated, sickly, but appreciative orphans. As his bottles clinked back and forth, he imagined that they were orphans and he was spiriting them to a safe haven where he would stand guard over them against the wily enemy.

His mother was always waiting with his hot breakfast when he returned from his valuable service. She was not privy to the motto that Peter lived and worked by, but she did know that she was a widow and only one child away from being childless. Many a night she awakened to hear Peter snoring in his room, and she was glad that she wasn't childless. Therefore, Peter had the attention of his mother more than most young men his age. He had never experienced what it was like to wash and press his own jacket and trousers, or to brush off his own hat, or even shine his own bicycle bell.

†

Now Brenda, in her misery of living as an orphan but without the privileges of friendship with other orphans, desired to escape from her loneliness and work in a place where she could belong. She wasn't averse to working. She didn't even mind serving others. She just hated loneliness.

Brenda's only solace was in books. When she read, she mostly noticed how fortunate the characters were to have friends. But one day she read an intriguing tale about a man stranded on an island, and it was a lonely existence until a ship arrived to save him. A year had passed since he had put the note in the bottle and thrown it out to sea. His rescuers had come, bearing the bottle and the note. Brenda sat musing on how blessed the stranded man was to be surrounded by a sea that could carry a message in a bottle to waiting rescuers. She wished that she had a sea to toss a bottle into. She wished that she just had a bottle. And then Brenda saw before her mind's eye the four crates of milk bottles that were delivered every day.

Under the watchful eye of Miss Crow, it was Brenda's job to make the daily exchange of milk bottles. But once the empty bottles were set outside the service door, no one else from the orphanage saw the empty bottles again. Late that night Brenda took pen in hand. With the image of Peter the milk deliverer in her mind, a piece of paper soon bore a message of desperation. The next morning just as Brenda heard the tinkle of the little bell, she set the crates down outside the door and pulled the paper from her pocket and quickly slipped it into the neck of a bottle.

Since on his approach to the orphanage Peter had heard a woman's harsh command and a window bang shut, he was already involved in an imaginary rescue operation. As he set down the new delivery and picked up the four jostling crates of empty bottles, he noticed the piece of paper tucked into one, but since he was making a getaway with a crate of 'orphans,' he didn't stop to investigate the paper until he was pedaling back toward the dairy. Then, in the manner of a soldier on the front line receiving a communiqué from a commanding officer, he took out the paper and read:

"To Whomever finds this bottle, I am being held against my will. Please have pity and rescue me. I will be indebted to you forever. If you can provide a way of escape, tie a string to one of the bottles in the bottom crate tomorrow. Signed, B."

The next morning Peter tied a string around one of the bottles, taking a large amount of care to tie it evenly. In a moment, all his years of living under the motto of Discipline, Dedication, and Determination were coming out of the imaginary and moving into reality. He delivered the milk with his reply in the bottom crate.

The day after that Peter could hardly wait to get to the orphanage where a true-life rescue operation was unfolding. His heart jumped when he saw another piece of paper. This one said:

"To my Rescuer, You will be rewarded for your kindness. Tell no one, but prepare a safe place to hide me. When you have prepared it, tie another string around a bottle in the top crate and come for me that night at midnight. Signed, B."

Peter was beside himself with feelings of importance. He was really going to carry out a rescue of a real orphan. In his mind he drew her picture. She was small and weak in spite of drinking the rickets-fighting milk he delivered. She was really a daughter of some wealthy land baron and had been kidnapped years ago. Her blond curls framed her face while her large trusting eyes looked up at him as he saluted in stiff military fashion. He tied the next string with extra care and even tied a bow to reveal the depth of his feelings.

Since Miss Crow held all orphanage keys herself and she alone controlled the comings and goings through the only two doors ever used — the main entrance and the service door — it is not surprising then that Miss Crow's sharp eyes did not miss the unusual string tied into a bow on the bottle in the center of the top crate. At first, and not making mention of it until it was snatched up by a thirsty girl, she menacingly accused that poor orphan of conspiracy; but when nothing could be confessed, Miss Crow then set her piercing gaze upon Brenda. But this was part of Brenda's larger scheme. She confidentially suggested to Miss Crow that perhaps one of the other orphans was planning an escape and this was the signal. Miss Crow's black eyes narrowed to mere pin pricks as she considered the unthinkable horror that one of her orphans would escape after they had willingly given thanks each night for the roof over their head, the food in their belly, and the clothes on their back.

To Brenda, Miss Crow asserted that it would never happen, and to make sure, she wanted Brenda herself to guard the door, with instructions that the ungrateful orphan should be nabbed and dragged immediately to Miss Crow's room, no matter the time of night. Brenda's escape was, therefore, in the offing.

All day Miss Crow favored her with the most hideous conspiratorial winks, and Brenda had to avoid looking at any of the orphans since she felt a faint tinge of guilt for implicating them. Patience until the hour of midnight was difficult to summon. Her small bag was packed and hidden in a kitchen cupboard. At sunset, she placed herself beside the door. As part of the plan, Brenda suggested to Miss Crow to leave the door unlocked so that the culprit could be apprehended in the very act of escape. Miss Crow hesitated, but concurred. Brenda's plan was complete.

Peter, in the meantime, had confided in his mother. The note said, "Tell no one," and he felt his mother was certainly not included in 'no one.' Besides, for him to bring the poor desperate orphan into their home as a safe haven, he needed for his mother to agree. Together they were busy all day making preparations for the soon-to-be-rescued captive. Peter occupied himself with his wagon where he would hide his blond and trusting orphan. His mother made up a tiny bed for her imagined frail and dainty waif. As she tucked in the sheet, she could almost feel those grateful arms around her neck. Her mother's heart was bursting in anticipation.

†

Brenda, however, sat by the orphanage door looking like neither of the images that were being concocted by her rescuers. She was an inch or two taller than Peter, and her hair was dark and straight, which she kept tied up in a net. Her eyes were quick and wary. She displayed none of the helplessness and meekness that both Peter and his mother expected.

Shortly before the appointed hour, Peter emboldened himself with his motto — Discipline, Dedication, Determination. He cycled through the dark town toward the orphanage at the even darker edge. His lips were set in a firm line to match his inward resolve to set a prisoner free even if he had to encounter the enemy which, at that time of night, took on all manner of forms and voices. But his imaginary adventure ended abruptly. Brenda met him as he pulled up to a stop. As soon as she stood by the wagon, she took charge.

Peter was not prepared to see the girl who set the bottles on the step. He was stunned to see her in place of his blond-haired lass. But when she said, 'Quick, hide me in your wagon,' he came around with military precision and remembered to do what he had planned. Before a full minute had passed, Brenda was hiding under a blanket where the milk crates usually were and Peter was pedaling back toward his house. Strangely, his motto was absent as he fell to wondering what happened to the kidnapped daughter of a rich man. When he felt they were far enough away from the orphanage and no one seemed to be pursuing them, he stopped pedaling and asked, "Are you the one who wrote those notes?" When Brenda answered, "Yes, and what do you think you're doing stopping before the safe haven?" Peter resumed pedaling and wondered even more deeply at how strange it was to feel none of the exhilaration he thought he would feel in the heat of a real rescue.

Peter's mother was waiting with a lamp lit and a pot of tea on the table. When she heard the sound of the bicycle, she smoothed her hair and her apron in readiness for being hugged by grateful arms. It was somewhat of a shock, therefore, when a dark-haired, able-looking girl stepped easily out of the wagon without needing any help from her gallant Peter. Peter came into the room still bearing his perplexity. Brenda came in shaking out her dress, mentioning the smell of milk in the cart, and Peter's mother looked on, rightly realizing there wouldn't be any comforting needed. She asked, "Are you the one who wrote the notes?" When Brenda answered, "Yes, and wasn't it a clever way to get out of that bondage?" Peter's mother couldn't think of anything to say.

Now that Peter and his mother had rescued Brenda, they had no thought to turn her out just because she didn't conform to their imagination. They had never rescued anyone before, so there was no idea of what to do next except to accept Brenda as a member of the household. Yet, neither Peter nor his mother felt any kind of tenderness toward Brenda. She needed no fattening up nor did she need succor.

As Brenda described life inside the orphanage and how it was that she came to be there, Peter and his mother were somewhat assured that they had truly helped to free a poor soul from a dirty and unpleasant place. Peter still felt sympathy for orphans because he was so close to being one, and Peter's mother felt sympathy for every child who needed mothered because she was so close to being childless, but neither could embrace Brenda as a third member of their family. They lived all together in a stilted harmony for some time, being bound together only because one had asked to be rescued and two had been willing to rescue. Peter belonged to his mother, and Peter's mother belonged to him, but Brenda belonged to neither.

Although she worked in the kitchen and made up the rooms each morning without complaint and even sat down to eat each meal with them like a member of the family, the day finally came when Brenda decided that she was as lonesome as before. She felt she had left one deserted island only to land on another. Brenda determined that she needed to be rescued once more. One day soon after that, the coal deliveryman found a note when he opened the coal chute that read, "Help me. I am being held against my will …"

♪

The Queen and Her Bee

Evil enforces fealty. Love grants freedom.

Once there was a buzzing yellow bee hard at work 'mong flowers of a tree, when all at once a blossom sucked him in, "Greetings there, my pollinating friend. Welcome to the Cherry Blossom Inn! Please have a seat, I'd like you to spend your life with me so that we can pretend that I'm a castle for you to defend."

Now, our buzzing bee thought very logically, concluding that nature works magically: since air rains water and water makes ice, miracles of nature never hide a vice.

"Sweet Cherry Flower, I am but a bee who works for the queen most diligently. Sure seems that a miracle in you grows, besides, the queen would never ever know if I don't return to that over-crowded hive, where she has a thousand men who've got no wives. So yes, my flower, let us join our lives!"

As any good reader can already see, such simple delights are not meant to be. Later that night the queen did attack and to her hive she brought him back. So, was it envy, or was it love, or was it the need to control from above? I dare not say, but the moral I'll sing:

"To cross a queen is a mighty foolish thing,
Be you a bee or be you a king."

ଓଃ

POISONED WATER

Evil lies to cripple others. Love reveals lies.

A little Spring sat alongside a path. She heard travelers coming and knew they were probably thirsty and that they would spy her and stop for a drink. Then they would say what all travelers said, "What's this! A dried-up spring! This map must be old. It shows a lush spot here, but look at this place. Everything is dead. Let's get out of here. I'll bet that spring has poisoned water."

These words hurt the little Spring as they were said over and over again by travelers who came upon her hoping for refreshment in their travels. She knew they had come a long way and from distant places, and it was her greatest desire to provide for them. When hands dipped water out of her basin and when backs leaned against her stones, she was her most content.

But when she heard the travelers say that she was poisoned, she knew it must be true. These travelers had seen so much of the world and they surely could tell the difference between a spring of good water and one of poison. However, the worst suffering of all was that she was helpless to give a drink to those who needed it.

In fact, water swirled down inside the little Spring. She could feel it splashing against her walls and she longed to send it up to the stone basin where it could collect and trickle down over the rocks, the way it used to be. She used to send out a steady flow and was admired for making the lushest spot on the map. And then one day she was cursed.

It was a witch who had laid the curse upon her. The witch hadn't even wanted a drink and wouldn't have even noticed her if not for the man. The witch had doubtlessly done some treachery to the man and he was trying to catch her in order to throw her into a dungeon where she belonged.

The little Spring remembers the day all too well. Just as the man was nearing the place where the little Spring bubbled, he doubled over with exhaustion, allowing the witch to increase the distance between them. The man found himself leaning against the Spring's stone basin and he quickly gulped three mouthfuls of water. In an instant, his strength was restored and he took off after the witch. The Spring had actually been pleased to see how well her water worked.

The man soon caught the witch and bound her hand and foot. He was carrying her back toward her deserved doom when the witch looked at the little Spring and cursed it for providing the man speed. "You are poison," she spat as she passed by.

The little Spring shuddered at these words. Her shudder shook a stone loose and it fell into her mouth. Instinctively she tried to dislodge the stone with a blast of water, but it was settled too firmly to budge. She realized with horror that it completely cut off her water. For the first time in her life the Spring did not flow.

The Spring couldn't imagine that the witch would curse her because she always had the best of intentions and would have given a drink to the witch as well as to the man. Desperately, she tried to forget what the witch had said. How could her water become poison? She was a bountiful spring with a well-known reputation for goodness.

But then she spied that stone stuck in her mouth. Why hadn't she been able to dislodge it? She was strong and robust, and besides, nothing had ever stopped her up before.

However, the words of the witch, "you are poison, you are poison," reverberated deeply within her, and then a light dawned for the Spring. A-ha, the witch may have cursed her, but the stone fell from above to prevent the Spring from poisoning anyone else. Therefore, the presence of the wedged stone gave the Spring comfort because inflicting another with her poison was as loathsome to the little Spring as refreshing the thirsty was pleasant.

She became glad for the stone, and each time she looked at it, she thanked it for keeping her poisonousness in. She even wondered if she could hide behind some vines or perhaps grow such a layer of moss that no travelers would notice her. Still, she wondered how long the curse would last and what she would do now that she couldn't give drinks to the thirsty. How would travelers understand that her lack of water was for their own good?

The wildflowers were the first to die. Next the grasses and then the bushes and finally the large tree that shaded her succumbed to drought. As the green growth browned, the little Spring knew she was surely poisoned and even her underground water was killing the plants from the roots upward. She began to despise the day that she had become a spring, and thus she sought for a way to flush the rancidness from within, but it remained and she felt stagnant.

With everything dusty and dead around her, the Spring lost all track of seasons and years and time. The only interruption to her destitution was the occasional traveler. Their spoken words of disappointment were a constant bane to the little Spring. When they called her "poison" and said, "Let's get out of here," her tears and her water became as one.

Secretly she hoped that one of the many travelers who passed would possess the answer to her dilemma. She hoped that her former reputation would inspire just one of them to look into the matter and have the magic solution. But none stopped long enough.

One day it began to rain with a most unusual vigor. It poured and it pounded and it washed all the dirt away from her stone basin and cleaned the rocks that hadn't had any water run over them for so long. The Spring wished a traveler would come by at that moment and think that the water in the basin was hers, but of course no one came.

The rainwater ran in torrents over the dusty ground, rushing past the little Spring with leaves and sticks and seeds. All that was left after the flash flood was an acorn that had come to rest in the mud a few feet away. The Spring spied the innocent acorn with horror and tried to shout out a warning to him that this was a dangerous place to grow. But he made no sign of having heard her and she watched him settle. The thought of killing one more living being was too much for the Spring. She closed her eyes and tried to die.

A very long time passed and all the maps were changed to reflect the Spring's area as a desolate stop — one to avoid being stuck at for a mealtime or for nightfall. For years travelers passed by and no one even expected to find a respite. As she slept, her dreams would hear in the pace of their steps "she's poison, she's poison."

Then one day the Spring felt something stirring her waters. Opening her eyes and looking around she saw a young Oak Tree shading her dry basin. She immediately cried, "Don't do that! My water is poisoned. You'll die."

"What do you mean poisoned? How can it be poisoned? Do you think I have grown up by drinking poison?"

The Spring had to nothing to say. She was surprised to see that the Oak Tree was large enough to give shade.

The tree went on, "Sorry if my roots startled you, but they have grown so long that every now and again I have to stretch them."

The Spring was urgently trying to reconcile what she was sure was true with what she saw and felt. There was obviously a sizeable Oak Tree where there had only been barren ground when she went to sleep. She looked around for another water source, perhaps a person carrying buckets, but saw nothing and no one.

"But I'm poison, I'm poison!" the little Spring repeated until the Oak Tree broke in and asked her why she kept saying that. Reluctantly, and with a great deal of shame, she told him the whole story from the beginning to the end, and made a most reverential mention of the stone that had miraculously fallen to keep her from polluting others.

The tree couldn't doubt the facts, for in truth, when he was just a small shoot, the area was barren and silent and desolate. And he didn't doubt that a witch had come by and said just what the little spring claimed. However, he also knew that it was a fact that he was well fed and had grown quickly on the Spring's water. The stone seemed the only dubious element.

After some thinking, the Oak Tree leaned over and took a look down into the Spring and saw the stone as it had lodged. It had certainly settled itself snugly, but it definitely didn't belong in the mouth of a spring. He saw that one of his branches could reach it, but he rightly assumed that poking at it would only lodge it more firmly. It seemed it had to be pushed from the inside out. Without saying what he thought about the stone, he began to talk.

He waxed lyrical about his dream to be a resting place for travelers and how interesting it would be to hear them talking about the many places in the world they had seen. He knew there were places he could never see because he was fixed into the ground, and so the only way to "visit" other places was to be visited by those who were not bound to one place. The little Spring was immediately captured by his dream. It had once been her way of life — bubbling and singing, refreshing the travelers, and hearing the tales of faraway places. While she was listening to the tree her waters began to roll back and forth underground.

The tree felt the movement with his roots and never let on, but continued to give voice to his latent dream. The more he talked, the more her waters stirred. He had been quiet for so long and so full of thoughts that he had no trouble describing his desire to be a resting place from many different vantage points.

All of a sudden there was a thunder down below and a stone went sailing up into the air and far out of sight. Water gushed out into the stone basin and down the rocks, sending a spray and a shower up through the branches of the Oak Tree, as if a long dormant geyser had awakened.

The little Spring was beside herself with surprise. What had happened was more by instinct than by effort. The tree, however, laconically commented that he thought that the stone had looked like it didn't belong.

The Spring was far over the edge of joy. She couldn't stop laughing. Water — pure, clean water — was cascading over her rocks and swirling in her basin and it wasn't poison after all! She had never been poison. With every new gush she said, "I am not poison! I am not poison!"

Before long, a group of travelers came up. They were consulting a map that was faded and dog-eared. "Ah, here it is," they said. "Here's the spring that Grandfather used to talk about. He was right, this makes the perfect resting spot. And look at that tree, too. Why don't we make our camp here! Let's spend the night."

Ever after that, the Spring and the Oak Tree became the favorite resting place for many travelers who told wonderful stories of faraway places while they sat under the tree's canopy. In time, all the maps were changed again and the spot was marked as the place to certainly spend a mealtime or be when night falls.

The Spring never did get over her good fortune of having the Oak Tree growing beside her. When smaller plants began to grow, they asked her to tell the story of her "poisoned water." With awe, she always recounted the part where she tried to get the Oak Tree to go away, first when he was an acorn, and then again when he was a shade tree; ironically, he was the only one who knew how to restore her life to her. And she always warned the small plants never to believe the words of a witch (which are most certainly always lies), because believing a lie makes the lie come true.

When no one was listening, the Oak Tree and the Spring spoke of many things. The Oak Tree told the little Spring of all the things he could see of the sky, and the little Spring told the Oak Tree of all the things she could see under the earth. Together they created one of the most extraordinary resting-places which all the passing travelers made mention of in their journals. They never forgot, however, that a witch could make a curse. They decided to still refresh all who stopped for a drink. But the tall Oak Tree spread out his roots far and deep against such a day when evil might strike again.

♪

Franklin P. Schmittie

Evil drives the prophets away.
Love can bring them back.

When Franklin P. Schmittie does walk in a room, the guys never laugh and the gals never swoon. All pull their heads back with their eyes open wide, thinking they're hiding what's hidden inside.

Now, Franklin P. Schmittie shows malice to none, it's just that he's able to know what they've done. He knows if the merchant has scales that are wrong, and knows which choir members don't live out their songs.

One day at a party while sipping some tea, the kingdom's First Lady did chat merrily. All those in the room gave her smiles of respect, all those except Frank who did in her detect a secret so guarded, a secret so clear, that when the First Lady did mingle too near to Franklin P. Schmittie, there rose up a fear inside her persona — her conscience was seared. Then squinting one cheek she gave Frank a blank grin, and Frank was ne'er asked to her parties again.

Still, Frank never aimed the clairvoyance he had intention'ly at folks to cause them to get mad. But had they the same skill that Franklin possessed, they'd use it to garner their own sweet success.

Since Franklin P. Schmittie held grudges to none, 'twas only one thing he could see to be done: he moved far away into hills where no roads brought anyone to him who casually strode. A man who can eas'ly tell what's right from wrong can never at parties dare hope to belong.

'Tis such a great pity that Frank moved away when really he has so much that he should say. Alas, dear Franklin, what else could you do? Yes, many are glad that you're far out of view. But some, plus one, do sorely miss you. Yes, Franklin P. Schmittie, we sorely miss you.

☙

The Bird Caller

Evil tricks and traps. Love redeems.

Beatrice loved birds. Her life was devoted to watching them, studying them, and collecting them. She didn't, however, collect them to let them live. She collected them in order to stuff them and mount them inside a glass case. Surely, she had a knack for making them look real even after their little quick eyes had been replaced by pieces of glass, and their living, breathing heart replaced by a wad of straw.

Her collection of rare birds had become quite well-known for its lifelike quality and amazing variety. Beatrice was proud that her Bird Sanctuary, as she called it, was acclaimed for its high caliber, and that none could boast a larger collection.

Once a year Beatrice made a special trip in order to increase her number of showcases. She inspired young men and women to accompany her, first in order to apprentice them in bird watching, but second, in order to use their many pairs of eyes and hands to fill more specimen bags than she could have done alone. In exchange for giving to her all that they gathered, Beatrice gave to each participant a gilt-edged certificate that could be hung on a wall to prove that they had advanced the study of birds.

Beatrice was recognized as the foremost expert on birds in her corner of the world. When she spoke about birds, everyone listened, and many were motivated to begin their own collections. Beatrice, however, guarded her own special taxidermy techniques of stuffing and posing the birds in lifelike positions, never allowing that information to be found out, for if it was, her own collection might be surpassed by another's. She felt she was doing quite enough to train young men and women in the arts of watching, studying, and bagging.

On a remote mountain in the southern hemisphere there lived a bird which Beatrice longed to have in her display. The bird's existence was more legendary than documented, but this only increased Beatrice's desire to have it. Sketchy references to the bird and its habits were found in ancient books which Beatrice had already paid dearly to obtain. She was so obsessed with whatever scanty information she could glean that she paid even more dearly for an antique map of the mountain where the bird lived, even though the map was of dubious accuracy. The map hung prominently in her Bird Sanctuary.

A man appeared one day and Beatrice immediately took an interest in him. He talked about the mountain, *the* mountain, as if he knew it intimately. He spoke about the flora and fauna of this remote peak as if they were as common as the rose and the field mouse. Not only was he familiar with the rare wildlife, he was adept at traversing the mountain. He knew it in the way that one knows the streets and alleys in a hometown. Beatrice had never imagined such a person existed.

Johnson was the man, and he thrilled large audiences with his knowledge of rare flowers and trees as well as his stories of strange birds. Then he mentioned the bird, the legendary bird. He had a book full of sketches illustrating its various behavior patterns. He had spent years making the drawings because there was only one bird (so he said) and it lived in the loneliest part of the mountain. Johnson could call the bird and it would come, but it was a magical ability that couldn't be duplicated in a wooden whistle, or even taught. He was the only one who had the ability to summon the bird. Others had come and tried in times past, but only Johnson was the possessor of the magic which called the bird and could keep it nearby.

Very soon he became known for his special knowledge, and there was great interest in how he survived on the mountain and, especially, how he had gained the ability to call the illusive bird. Johnson could not tell how it was he could call the bird. The skill had been with him always. He had never been taught it. This aspect increased the interest in hearing his tales, and when Beatrice realized her expert knowledge of birds was being supplanted by his stories and magical ability, she quite naturally became jealous.

She invited Johnson to see her collection of stuffed birds. She meant to impress him by the real-to-life portrayal of so many birds of the world, for she felt she had to prove that she was a bird expert worthy of his help. But Johnson had little appreciation for birds which were kept behind glass. Beatrice saw that Johnson wasn't impressed by her vast display, so she added contempt to her jealousy.

The map on the wall of the mountain caught Johnson's eye instead. Beatrice noticed that Johnson noticed the map. She allowed no time to elapse before extolling the unique bird that was there to be studied, craftily omitting that the bird was there to be collected. For an hour, Beatrice sang the praises of the small winged creature. By the time she was finished, she had convinced Johnson that she only longed to see it with her own eyes and draw pictures of it for scientific books, which was also one of her occupations.

So it was, based on the belief that Beatrice wanted to draw the solitary bird, that Johnson agreed to assist her. Before he left her gallery that day, plans were made for him to meet her and her group at the small village at the base of the mountain in exactly three months' time. Although Johnson couldn't tell anyone else how to call the bird, he could tell them what kinds of clothes to wear and what kinds of food and medicines to bring, which he detailed for Beatrice.

Johnson made the long journey back to the mountain, and in the ensuing months, devised a plan to give Beatrice and her group plenty of chances to observe the bird. He paid close attention to choosing trails that were easy to follow and camp spots that were close to water. The appointed day neared and Johnson set off down the mountain. He gave himself an extra day so that he could gather supplies in the village and be rested for leading a group of novices.

Before he reached the bottom, however, Beatrice and her group arrived in the village that marked the way onto the mountain. Beatrice knew fully well that they were early and she knew the risk she was taking, but it had so bothered her that Johnson's stories about the bird had drawn such crowds and stunted her own expert status that she told her group that Johnson was late. The group of followers hadn't been privy to the original agreement. They believed her thoroughly.

Before setting off as her own guide, Beatrice told everyone she saw in the village that Johnson, that wilderness man who probably doesn't even own a watch or a calendar, was late, and as she had a deadline to meet, she was forced to start off on her own. The villagers advised her against it, but Beatrice stubbornly refused to stay in the village and lose a single day on the mountain. She led her followers, not up the mountain at that point, but around it, wanting to give Johnson a bit of a chore to find and catch up to them.

Naturally, Johnson arrived in the village a day ahead of schedule only to be met with the incomprehensible news that the group was there and gone. They had already started off around the mountain the day before, which was especially alarming since the course around the side of the mountain was dangerous, filled with unmapped pitfalls.

Setting off just as he was, with his bag packed but not balanced, Johnson traced the steps of Beatrice and her flock. Night came on and he still had not caught up to them, and though he felt it was unsafe to walk in the darkness, he feared what peril might befall them if he wasn't their guide. Using the light of the half moon he walked on through the night.

It wasn't until noon of the next day that he caught up to them. It would have taken even longer if one of their number hadn't sprained an ankle. Johnson was confounded by the speed at which they had traveled to get to that point. For the moment, he attributed it all to their enthusiasm for getting a look at the bird. Even when Beatrice welcomed him as their tardy guide, he didn't suspect that she was intending to give him trouble.

Johnson was made responsible for the sprained ankle and the group's general low morale before he knew what was going on. Beatrice berated him for being late and throwing their whole adventure off by a full day and maybe more. Her followers looked at their erstwhile guide with admiration. But Johnson was commanded to lead them now and try to make up for the trouble he had already caused, which meant carrying the one with the sprained ankle on his back.

Johnson was so used to living among the wildlife and dwelling in a silent world of thoughts and senses that he assumed that he had done something wrong in the world of people and talk, but it would take some time to puzzle out just what it was he had done. When he took his place in the front to lead the way up the mountain, he turned over in his mind the details as he and Beatrice had worked them out, and he could not figure that he was late.

Before Johnson could get to the place where he had planned to call the bird, Beatrice began to lead the group off to the side. She claimed to have heard the bird calling. Johnson frequently found himself carrying the wounded traveler, but not leading anyone else. By the time he found where the rest had turned off, they had gone too far away from the easy trail. Backtracking would have delayed them more. Johnson found himself leading the group on rugged trails, quite suitable for himself, but difficult for the rest. Behind him, Beatrice kept up a steady complaint about the trail until she claimed to have heard the bird calling again and made her way toward it, guiding the rest behind her. Thus it went all the way up the mountain. She half-jokingly asked Johnson if he was taking so long to call the bird just to make her and her group appear to be softies.

Of course, they were all convinced that he was withholding calling for the bird for some secret self-serving reason. Even if Beatrice and the group could believe Johnson knew some sort of magical call, they certainly believed that magic was a sort of art that could be performed on the spot, and not to perform it was a matter of choice. That the magic would only work when a set of unexplainable conditions were in place completely was beyond their understanding.

Johnson knew the set of conditions which were needed to not only call the bird but for the bird to show itself, yet, he had never had to put it into words before. He could not explain it now. He assumed that Beatrice and her group would trust his inborn ability and be more patient. Therefore, he had no response to make to Beatrice's thinly veiled accusations. Just as his ability to call the bird was inborn, so was his *inability* to defend himself.

The whole group was irritated with fatigue and with itching from bug bites. Beatrice had also kept from them the list of the most useful ointments to bring. When Beatrice laid all the blame onto Johnson, it seemed justified since this mountain was his abode and he was the only one not scratching. Inwardly, Beatrice gloried in all the discomforts of her and her followers because it gave her ample ways to be revered as a better guide and bird watcher than Johnson.

Johnson, still under the impression that the group wanted to sketch the bird, went off to a quiet place far from the noise of the irritated followers of Beatrice and called for the bird. It was a longer time in coming than he had ever experienced before, but finally it fluttered to the ground where Johnson was kneeling. He coaxed the bird to wait by scattering some of its favorite seeds on the ground as a reward.

In disbelief, the group followed Johnson along the mountain trail. He was clearly enthusiastic about showing them the bird, and it rankled Beatrice that his confidence hadn't been thwarted by her crafty diversions. He was, once again, showing himself to be more expert than she in the matter of birds.

Holding up his hand for silence as they approached the place where the lone bird was pecking at seeds on the ground, Johnson was like a proud father showing off his new son. He stood waiting for the sketchpads to be taken out and the sound of pencils on paper to begin. But there was nothing of the sort.

Before Johnson could suspect it or prevent it, one of the members slapped a net over the bird and killed it. With happy cheers, Beatrice's group celebrated catching the bird. This act of fatal deceit made Johnson now clearly understand what, up to then, he had only felt. With his ire piqued, he announced the descent was beginning at that moment, and if any hoped to get off the mountain, they had but one chance to follow him, now. There was a scramble of activity as the followers of Beatrice tried to pack up, for no one disbelieved Johnson. His sudden fury had convinced them all.

After a long confusion of identical-looking trails, they came to the bottom of the mountain. Beatrice had tried to goad Johnson into explaining himself and his sudden impulse to hurry them off the mountain, but he refused to answer or respond to her recriminations. At the bottom, he turned around without further conversation and headed back up his mountain.

Beatrice smugly explained to her followers that he was merely jealous because she had done what he never had been able to do — bag the bird. The followers believed her because they were itching and tired, and it seemed the only explanation for such a sudden outburst of fury, for the original agreement to only draw the bird was also kept from them.

Beatrice added the rare bird to her collection in a glass case built just for it. She labeled the glass case "male." With her ambition heightened by owning this prize, she prepared and labeled another case "female," assuming she could obtain a pair.

The next year she sent off a group of young men and women to collect the female on their own, claiming she had something very important to do at that very time and, therefore, couldn't go herself. She knew Johnson would never agree to lead her up onto the mountain again. However, she had made a crude map from memory using the antique map as a reference with the approximate spot marked where the male bird was captured, and she assured the young men and women that they would successfully find the female bird if they followed her map carefully. She did warn them not to have anything to do with that wilderness man Johnson because he was an impulsive sort and couldn't be trusted.

Just as Beatrice kept her techniques of stuffing a secret, so she supposed that Johnson had kept his method of finding the bird a secret. She had never believed that it was magic that called it. Also, she had never believed that there was only one solitary bird. Now that she knew its location, she had no doubt about bagging the female.

After their long journey, the group of young men and women approached the mountain but soon found themselves hopelessly lost. They had wandered in circles for days when Johnson found them. He was startled to find such a group on the mountain and immediately offered to help them find their way off. They distrusted him thoroughly because of Beatrice's instructions and assured him that they knew where they were and how to leave the mountain.

As Johnson had no grounds to say they had to leave, he left them and went on his own way. But several days later he came upon them again and they were in worse condition than before. Some of them were wounded and one was deathly ill. Johnson noticed the map lying on the ground that Beatrice had made for them with the place marked where the male bird had been netted. He picked it up and slowly shook his head over it. With gentle persuasion, he told the group that they had been misled to think they could find the bird just by looking for it, and besides, such a sketchy map would never get them off the mountain. Because one of their number was so ill, they allowed Johnson to lead them down the mountain.

In the village, Johnson made arrangements for the one who was near death to be taken care of and for the others to have their wounds treated. The people in the village trusted Johnson and were amazed that he was showing such concern for such outsiders greedy with wanderlust.

It took some time for the group to make the long journey home, and the families who were anxiously awaiting their return went to see Beatrice to inquire what was keeping them. Beatrice explained to them that the group had the best of maps to follow as well as her own good example from the previous trip, so if they had not returned, it was only because of mistakes and hazards which she had nothing to do with. But she assured them that everything would be just fine.

The group, however, which had been making its way back unbeknownst to their families or to Beatrice, was coming up behind her just as she was in the middle of reminding the crowd about that rascal who lived on the mountain who was so untrustworthy on the previous expedition, and that it is possible he might have tricked the group into getting lost. It was awkward for Beatrice that they appeared from behind, but without missing a beat, her face turned to all smiles and she welcomed them home with the warmest of words. She even masked her surprise at seeing Johnson among them. As if to revel in this moment of success while all eyes were on her, she asked to see the female bird they had brought. The group turned in unison toward Johnson. Beatrice seethed inside that he would dare to once again steal her glory.

Johnson produced no bird but began to tell a story. The bird, he began, was special and rare because it was not originally a bird but another being that had turned into a bird and lived a life of solitude on the mountain. There was no such thing as an egg from this bird, he continued, because the male and female did not mate. In fact, only one bird of either gender lived on the mountain at any one time. For, above all else, the being that inhabited the body of the bird was to live without companionship. The being, Johnson revealed, was a person who had abused the trust of others to such an extent that he or she was no longer worthy to occupy the human body. As a punishment, the soul had to become a bird that flew away to live on the remote mountain until it met a natural death. Johnson had become the bird's only company.

Regarding a female bird, Johnson said there hadn't been one on the mountain for a while, but he did say that he was sure that one due to come soon. Then, at the very moment he said those words, Beatrice gave out a muffled peep as her arms turned to feathers and her nose to a beak. She shrunk into a small nervous bird. One of the bird watchers standing behind Johnson immediately clapped a net over the bird.

Johnson continued by saying that since these rare birds hold the soul of a person, however wicked in life, he wished to take the male that had been captured and give it a proper burial on the mountain where it had died. Johnson's eyes then turned to the glass case which had been prepared for the female. All eyes followed his. He turned to the one holding the net and quietly said, "Let her fly free. The mountain is calling."

♪

ON EDGE OF WOODS

Evil keeps the rat race going. Love steps outside it.

I am a lonely wanderer alone on edge of woods that form a fragile last defense 'gainst urban neighborhood.

Through trees I watch a passing car — her jaw is set and raised; she speeds past with an urgency I knew in younger days. She's got a meeting, then a date (her "ex" has got the kids). But after dinner, there's no dance. She needs to shut her lids.

The faces through the trees I see do keep me walking on: they run the race of cold success which I am loath to join. I am one lonely wanderer, but I am not alone. Widows, prophets, poets know that edge of woods as home.

03

Shipwrecked

Evil labels and scapegoats.
Love is beyond such control.

"Look at her hands. She can't have been a first-class passenger. She must have been in steerage."

"Calloused hands don't mean low class. The calluses may be a result of some hobby of the rich. I look at her hair and say, with those kinds of locks, she must have been a first-class passenger."

"You're both looking at the problem too narrowly. I look in her eyes and I see someone who has known pain, and not just the kind of being tossed into the sea, if you take my meaning. I think she was running away from something or someone, and that leads me to think she was a stowaway."

A young woman lying on a hospital bed mutely followed this conversation with her eyes, stopping on each woman's face as she spoke. Her face registered nothing in response to their observations. As the sole survivor of a ship that had caught fire and exploded a mile from port, she was the center of attention.

The ship was returning from a port in the South. It was a routine and well-trusted route since it did not have to cross the sea. That it ended in catastrophe had the whole country in an uproar. The shipping route was a favorite of the wealthy. It shortened a long overland journey between their two favorite cities to a mere three days. The lower classes enjoyed it as well since they could pay a low fare to reach a city where they might find employment. The ship itself provided employment for numerous stewards, cooks, baggage handlers, and musical bands, for it was not to be three days without entertainment and good food for those who could pay.

For days, the report had been that all passengers and crew alike had perished in the blaze and explosion. But then a fisherman had come across an unconscious woman floating upon a piece of wreckage and covered only with a piece of tarp. When this was reported, all the relatives and friends of the passengers and crew converged on the hospital where the woman had been taken.

Hopes had been dashed that the woman herself would provide any clues when it was discovered that she could talk but had lost her memory, and she possessed nothing on her person as identification. As she was in need of medical attention due to being exposed for three days in the sea without food or drink, a Committee of three women was thus gathered around her bed to begin their task. They had been called together by the mayor of the city to which the ship was destined and he commissioned them to use all their powers of observation and knowledge of humankind to help identify this woman and restore her to her family, or to whatever she deserved.

The fortunate — or rather, unfortunate — woman who lay upon the bed might just as well have perished in the shipwreck as to be subjected to what awaited her. Her survival seemed too miraculous for her to be allowed to slip into the oblivion of her waiting family, not to mention that she was the only witness to what possibly might have been the cause of the explosion. Many were interested in her identity, but a few were obsessed with what she might know.

The mayor of the city fell into both categories. When he received news that one had survived, he ordered a tight security cordon placed around the hospital. The nurses and doctors in her ward were given paid leave and replaced with ones of his own choosing. The fisherman was tracked down and given a new boat and a large pension just to relocate and forget what he saw. Before any description of the woman was released — either a sketch of her face or a description in print — the mayor announced to the press that she was burned beyond recognition and suffered acute amnesia, and, therefore, he would appoint a Committee to find out her identity which would take time but would, in the end, restore her to her proper loved ones.

By way of legitimizing his approach, he told those three women of the Committee that if she turned out to be the heiress who was allegedly on board, a sinister sort might try to claim her as his wife and then hold her for ransom. He bristled at the idea that such a scandal would occur during his tenure as mayor.

The Three were aware that the woman's face was not burned beyond recognition, but they trusted the mayor to have some superior wisdom in saying so to the press. He seemed intent on borrowing time before there was a demand from the crowd outside the hospital doors to view the woman and settle the mystery.

Toward the end of each day, the Committee of Three stood on the hospital steps facing the sea of upturned faces to give an update on what they had observed.

"We have observed that this is a young woman not more than thirty years old, but we have noticed an indentation on her left ring finger, so we can surmise only that she was married, or had been married, or was perhaps engaged."

"Furthermore, she has good looks, well, a-hem, that is, if you discount the damage done by exposure and burns. She bears no distinguishing characteristics or birthmarks."

"We have discovered that she responds when she hears certain words, but we will keep that information to ourselves until we have done a thorough investigation to protect all of you from false hope and further heartache."

At this information, some in the crowd turned away, but the rest pressed closer and shouted out questions and suggestions until the hospital doors were firmly closed with the Three safely on the other side.

These Three were sharply divided over their observations. One by one around the hospital bed, they made their cases:

"I say a person can be identified by their physical characteristics. Observe the strong muscles in her arms and her well-used feet. This is no idle heiress. This woman has known work and activity. That jaw is not a proud one."

"But notice her straight teeth and delicate earlobes. Surely, this is the face of a noble woman who inherited a touch of humility, perhaps from her mother's side. I contend that the strong arms and strong legs indicate not manual labor, but that she could ride horses. That puts her in the category of the wealthy."

"Neither of you two look deeply enough. I say that physical characteristics can be misleading. Notice how she looks when I say 'music, money, men, and magic.' She widens her eyes, and in them, I can see great hurt and past abuse."

At intervals they each would lean over and ask, "What is your name? Where are you from? Can you remember anything about the explosion on the ship?" To all these questions, the woman would shake her head.

She allowed the daily examinations and discussions because she couldn't do otherwise. In actuality, she had survived her trauma without much bodily damage and could have gotten out of bed and walked to the front of the hospital to see who among the crowd identified her, but the mayor forbade it, arranging that she be kept sedated and under strict watch until a positive identity was made.

"I tell you, I think our job is as good as done. We should just announce that she was one of the multitude going to find domestic employment and let her lie here until her memory comes back."

"Not so. My opinion, after examining her whole physique, is that she might be the heiress who was known to be on the ship.

We can't let her lie. We must carry out our commission with all of our skill, for you know, there will be a reward from her father — if she is the heiress — when we help to restore his daughter."

"But I ask you, what kind of person would be the only one to survive such an explosion? Surely, we are dealing with a person who has lived a life by her wits and knows how to escape when trouble arrives."

Thus the women went on around the bed for days, observing, contending, inspecting, and grappling to solve the mystery. When they had formed their opinions, the mayor paid a visit to the hospital. He waded through the crowd of hopeful relations, and with smiles and handshakes, promised to do his best to settle the woman's identity.

His pleasant manner concealed that a few days before he had received two pieces of information. The first could be the downfall of his term as mayor and end his career in ignominy. The other, fortunately, could be used to prevent that awful turn of events.

He faced his Committee of Three and asked for their results.

"Mr. Mayor, I say without a doubt that we can tell all the common people to stay and promise that she belongs to one of them."

"On the contrary, Mr. Mayor, I say we can tell the crowd to disperse except for those who are waiting in their carriages. I am positive she comes from the privileged class."

"Now, Mr. Mayor, you and I have both known trials and disappointments, contrary to these other two here, and so I know that if you had looked into her eyes, as I have done, you would agree that we should tell everyone to go home — that the woman doesn't want to be found."

The mayor leaned forward and drew the three heads to come near his. In a whisper that oozed with conspiracy, he told them, "I have just received secret intelligence that confirms that a con woman of superior talent boarded the ship at the Southern port.

She is known to have swindled many an old man out of his fortune and to be a master of disguise as well. No one knew in what guise she would appear, so now you know why I couldn't allow this woman to be seen. I hope you will forgive me for keeping you in the dark; her cohorts could have easily claimed her as their kin and helped her escape from justice."

The three woman each exchanged looks of understanding with the mayor and glanced sideways at the woman in the bed.

"*Oh, I quite see it now. A woman of that persuasion couldn't hide the rough side of her nature when her calloused limbs and her commonly shaped jaw are left undisguised.*"

"*To be sure, she would have cultivated her looks to match that of a well-to-do woman in order to ensnare her wealthy victims. I see that she may surely ride horses as an expert, but yes, certainly more as a means of getaway than as a hobby or sport.*"

"*Now for once I can agree with you both. I saw it in her eyes, didn't I? She has the look of one who can con and pretend, and yet beguile you with a smile.*"

The mayor was glad that they were cooperating with his need to pin an identity on this woman. Without the public ever needing to see her, she could be labeled and sent to her punishment. The mayor kept the other bit of intelligence to himself at the moment. When it came to light, it wouldn't be difficult to say as well that this woman, this conniver, this fraud, and this thief, was surely at the crux of it.

The woman in the bed had lost her memory, but she hadn't lost her conscience or her perception of right and wrong. The conspiratorial nature of the mayor and the three women and their sidelong glances did not escape her. Their looks frightened her, and she knew from her days under their inspection that she could expect no help from them. Was there no one whose hand she could grab and plead for help? Only they came near. The room was sealed off.

With their job completed, the mayor dismissed the Committee and paid them handsomely for their invaluable help. He himself went to bring in his Chief of Police. The time was right.

As the mayor knew, the story would be broken in today's newspaper that he had been involved in a smuggling ring which only came to light when certain items were found floating amid the wreckage of the ship. The evidence against him would be harmful, but he planned to insist that he was innocent of wrongdoing and that the real criminal lay in the hospital hoping to escape justice by feigning amnesia and loss of identity. It was well established that the con woman who boarded at the Southern port was capable of framing him. Who wouldn't believe that she had been the one that struck the match that started the blaze that caused the explosion that took so many innocent lives? And didn't it make sense that she was the only one to survive? The cause of the blaze and explosion was still a mystery, so it was up to the mayor to invent the scenario.

His plan may well have worked, for all the friends and relations had only his word and the word of the Committee to go on. But in the commotion of the Committee departing and the mayor leaving to fetch the Chief, the woman was left alone in her room. When the commotion had died down, a young girl came in to do the floors. She hadn't been intending to do wrong, but there was no one in the room to keep her out. When the young girl came near the bed, the shipwreck survivor fought her grogginess and grabbed the girl by the wrist and got out only two words, "Help Me!" In that instant, the girl with the mop was forced to look into the woman's eyes and to see her face. The fierceness of the woman's grip and the surprise of being grabbed caused the young mopping girl to cry out. Her cry brought a nurse who scolded, "How dare you come into this room! This is the room of the shipwreck survivor. Didn't I tell you to mop all rooms but this?"

The girl, although she only mopped floors, was not stupid. It occurred to her that she had heard that the survivor was burned beyond recognition. The look of the woman's face and the pleading in her voice tormented the girl. As she had been brought up by honest parents who insisted on complete and unwavering truthfulness, she now felt herself to be part of a lie.

The nurse, swearing her to silence, sent her home and told her not to return until the next week if she hoped to keep her simple job. The mopping girl agreed. But on her way home as she passed the friends and relations keeping vigil outside, she noticed a man sitting on the curb weeping into his hands. The memory of the woman pleading for help combined with the sight of this man weeping bitterly were too much for a pure heart to ignore, no matter the cost.

Being simple and straightforward, she told the man in a few words that she had seen the face of the woman who survived the shipwreck and that she lay alone in a room in the back of the hospital. The man listened in stunned silence to the description of hair color and eyes, and at once decided to find a way around the security cordon.

The simple mopping girl felt she had done what she could and if the woman didn't belong to that man, the message would at least get around that the survivor was recognizable. The girl was rewarded enough by seeing the look of gratitude in the weeping man's eyes, but if she had known just how much treachery she was preventing, she would have been willing to sacrifice much more than her job.

The man hadn't been able to believe that his fiancée was drowned in the bottom of the sea. He had waited during those days, clinging to every word from the three women, and hope wouldn't die. But when he saw the Committee leave with no a final announcement and the mayor scurry off with a look of urgency, he lost all hope and sat down to finally cry and mourn the loss of his soon-to-be bride.

They had met in India as single missionaries, and though they immediately wished to marry, they were required to finish their five-year terms before returning to their homeland to marry. He had left earlier than she to make arrangements and find a humble dwelling. Leaving her behind had caused him anxiety, but he imagined the dangers to be malaria or a tiger. Never had he considered that the last leg of the journey — a trusted domestic route — would take her away from him. He wished he had perished with her. It was at this point that the gentle voice of the mopping girl interrupted his sobs of grief.

He needed no more encouragement than that the survivor could be viewed. With courage from his renewed hope, he eluded the security cordon and scaled the wall. It was a tedious task to peek unseen into the windows, but at last he came to the window of the shipwreck survivor. As his eyes came up above the windowsill, he met her eyes gazing forlornly out the window. In that meeting of the eyes, her memory was instantly restored. She put up the window and he crawled in. They embraced, awash in tears.

They would have reveled in their joy longer, except the man couldn't forget the disquieting look of the mayor as he had left the hospital, and he began to wonder about the reason for the lie; so he found something for his fiancée to wear and he resolutely guided her through the hospital corridors, ignoring the warnings by the hospital staff to stop.

Just as they approached the front doors, they heard the mayor accompanied by a squad of police trying to disperse the crowd by announcing that the mystery had been solved and that the Chief of Police himself had come with him to personally carry away the criminal — a criminal who not only had swindled many a gentleman and even attempted to frame him, the mayor, in a crime, but was the very person responsible for blowing up the ship! To hear this unpleasant news after all the days of waiting and hoping increased the agitation of the crowd.

Without the mayor being aware, the doors behind him opened and there stood the man who had been weeping and the woman who had survived the shipwreck. The eyes of the crowd moved as one from the mayor and his law enforcers to the faces of the happy man and woman. The crowd recognized the man as one who had bided the long days among them, and the unnaturally dressed woman coming with him from inside the hospital fulfilled their suspicion that they had been lied to and were being lied to at that very moment. As they felt wronged themselves, their passion increased.

The mayor turned to see what was behind him. He felt himself suddenly surrounded. The police sensed the delicate nature of this confrontation and were unsure which side to take, but there was no need for them to act. The crowd itself, in fury, apprehended the mayor and moved off toward the harbor's edge.

The reunited couple was left standing upon the hospital stairs. The man turned to his fiancée and quietly observed, "India has no dangers to match a Committee."

♪

Corn Trees in Autumn

Evil offers false security. Love is security.

It wasn't the first thing I saw that day — to tell you that first would cause you dismay. The first thing I met was an Ear of Corn op'ning her curtains to greet the new morn. Shaking her tassels, she let out a yawn. (To let out a yawn? An Ear that can yawn?)

Right under her cottage was a Beetle who winked, inviting me over to share in a drink of droplets of dew which did make him to sing. (Though who can imagine a Beetle that sings?) But tune was cut short. I lifted my claw, ready to run from the third thing I saw — a Monster Machine making corn trees fall! (They seemed until then so strong and so tall.)

Alas, it was time to find a new hole; seems corn woods are not so safe for a mole. I think now I know why they call autumn fall, because when it comes, it befalls one and all.

The Icemaker's Family

Evil tells us we're worthless. Love has a big job.

It was raining outside, but there was no need to place a bucket here or there to catch drips from the ceiling. The farmhouse of the ice maker's family was soundly constructed. The family was sitting inside before a modest fire, drinking hot mulled cider and talking about the end of their ice gathering season. They had just gotten the icehouse filled before the rain started.

The family boasted four boys — the oldest already as strong as a full-grown man and the youngest just learning to read. On this evening as the rain was falling, the talk around the fire centered upon the recent exploits of getting the ice cut and stored.

The oldest recalled the dangers of his job out on the ice, cutting with the long saw, attaching the hooks, guiding the ice out of the water onto the sled. The next countered with how tricky it was to keep the team of horses working, going back and forth between the lake and the block house, especially keeping them from slipping on the ice. The third, facing heavy competition from the first two, extolled his feat of getting the ice stacked — both deep and high — in the icehouse where he was the last one to touch it before it would be called forth in the spring and summer. Properly stacked ice was essential since it would be noticed when the first deliveries to customers began to be made.

The fourth and youngest felt he had done something, as well, to contribute to the process, but since layering hay around and on top of each ice block was neither strenuous nor dangerous, he had done nothing to merit boasting. As each older brother boasted about his own worth in the ice gathering process, the youngest stayed mute and dreamed of doing what they had done.

He had watched the oldest manage the saw and hooks, and had seen him nearly lose his footing a time or two but regain it just in time. He had listened to the second oldest give instructions to the horses and had watched him back them onto the lake and keep them still while the blocks were loaded. As the horses pulled the load into the icehouse, he had seen the third brother take charge of the blocks, handling his particular job with precision and gravity. The youngest brother had often been accused of getting in his way, hampering exactly how well the ice blocks could be stacked.

The youngest brother secretly imagined himself stacking the ice just as exactly as his next oldest brother, if not more exactly. He imagined himself driving the team of horses in all their maneuvers just as well as the next brother, if not better. Finally, he imagined himself cutting and lifting out the ice from the lake as expertly as the oldest brother, if not more expertly. He imagined that his own feet would never slip.

The presence of the father in all these various stages of ice cutting and storage went completely unobserved by the youngest brother. The youngest brother only saw the brothers and knew that he would never get to do the jobs they were doing because he was the youngest.

While he waited in the icehouse to spread the hay, he would sometimes invent ways that he could be promoted, such as, the older brother falling into the lake and having to be put to bed to recover. Then all the brothers would move up the ladder with himself taking over the ice-stacking job. Or sometimes, he imagined that the brother who drove the horses got stepped on and was temporarily lame, and a smart boy was needed to fill in and call out the commands to the team. In his wildest dream, however, he got promoted out to the lake itself to work the saw and attach the hooks because the brother who did the stacking, dropped a block on his foot, and the older two brothers had to move down the ladder, while he jumped into the top spot. But he knew this last dream was the most unlikely.

While the brothers sat around the crackling fire with the rain falling outside and hot cider being ladled out, the youngest brother listened to the deeds of his older brothers and heard the way each rivaled his skill against the skills of the others. He knew that he would get laughed out of the room if he called attention to the way he had layered the straw so evenly and carefully between the blocks. When deliveries began to be made, no one would stop to notice how nicely the straw was layered. It would be summarily brushed away with no thought given to his own contribution. Still, he knew his own work was valuable, but it took no muscles, and it wasn't dangerous.

Years went on in this way with each brother performing his particular job in the ice cutting and storing process. Then there came a war, not in their land but across the sea. The three older brothers went to join the war, and only the youngest was left at home. With them gone, there was no longer any need to invent ways that he could do the brothers' jobs. He did them all, plus his own, with his father working beside him. But that year when the rain came and the season for cutting the ice was over, there was no one to drink mulled cider with and compare danger and skill.

One day the war was over and the brothers returned. They sat around the fire drinking the cider and talked about their exploits in the war. The oldest one talked about routing the enemy and taking a valuable hilltop. The next oldest one had been wounded, but not before blowing up the enemy's ammunition dump. The third oldest, faced with such heavy competition, recounted his daring feat of escaping from a prison camp. And the youngest remained quiet. He knew that he would be laughed out of the room if he called attention to the way he had been cutting and storing the ice.

♪

PAPER DRAGON

Evil denies loss. Love embraces loss.

The little old man by the road had a stand to sell paper dragons, each cut by his hand. Their colors were yellow and purple and green. Their bones were of bamboo which made them all seem like Festival lanterns, except for one thing: inside was no place for a candle to rest.

And yet from their nostrils, as you might've guessed, spit fire like a torch for a second or two, then, up in the air, Dragon's paper all blew. So quickly the splendor of paper did burn; colors and shapes into ash and smoke turned. Only charred bamboo was left on the ground, with no trace of Dragon to ever be found.

One day a girl (who was soon to meet death) did stop by his stand to make one small request: "Hello, Mr. Dragon-man, O pretty please, light up a dragon especially for me. I have no pennies to buy one from you, but please light that green one with eyes baby blue."

The joy in her eyes as the dragon spat fire was treasure enough for the man to retire. But later that day into danger she strayed, and now deep in China her body is laid.

Still, knowing the joy of the dragon's bright flame was last in her mind when her short life was claimed does comfort the hearts of the ones who are left. It eases the pain though they still live bereft.

That light flickers bright and will light up my eye until my last day when I also shall die. The torch from the dragon — just second or two — eternally burns, as I've shared it with you.

The Chinese Laundry

Evil looks for easy gold. Love labors for it.

A long time ago in the hills of California gold was found just waiting to be mined. It was twinkling in the rocks and riverbeds, winking back at the sun. When word leaked out that gold had been found, there was a mighty rush of men who came seeking their fortunes. These were the hardiest of men — the most willing to give up civilization and, therefore, the least likely to see the need to be clean.

To get to California these men had to travel great distances. They had to travel light and travel fast to get there first because no one knew how long the gold would last. In their haste, the men brought only the necessities: a blanket to sleep in, a pan to cook in, tools for mining, and bags to drop gold pieces into; but they left behind all frivolities, such as anything to wash their clothes with.

Of course, the work of a miner was very dirty work. Either they were chipping away the sides of a mountain with a pickax all day or sloshing through a muddy stream to pan for flecks of gold. Naturally, the clothes of the miners got filthy.

Only once a month or so did the miners leave their claims to go to town where they had the gold weighed and exchanged for money. When they did this, they formed a very dirty bunch of miners, but no one noticed anyone else's dirtiness because they were all dirty the same.

There was one person, however, who did notice the dirt, and this was Hong Shou. He was a Chinese man who had also come to California to seek his fortune, but he was not allowed to stake a claim. According to the law of that time, he could only do the undesirable work. Therefore, his gold mine lay in the dirtiness of the miners' clothes. He opened up a clothes washing service in the town where the miners came to have their gold pieces weighed. His big caldron for boiling water was sitting in all readiness to receive the dirt-encrusted shirts and trousers of the miners. He had a big paddle ready to stir them around and knock the mud out of the fibers. He had lines of rope strung between trees to hang them out to dry.

But business for Hong Shou was terribly slow. Occasionally, a miner would take off his shirt and his dungarees and allow Hong Shou to make them clean, but the miner would never take off his long johns. He would sit and wait in his red one-piece undergarment and feel as good as naked doing it. Regardless of the fact that the long johns could stand up by themselves, the miner couldn't bear the thought of parting with what was as good as his own skin.

Even though his caldron stood unfilled and his lengths and lengths of rope hung empty, Hong Shou didn't give up hope of finding gold in the dirt of the miner's clothes. But the miners did not care about being clean, and so Hong Shou's business remained terribly slow.

One day, Hong Shou had an idea. He considered it from every angle. Here was a camp of miners. They were all wealthy from the gold mines. They weren't a bad sort, although some of them did fight and brawl once in a while. They worked hard. Some were even handsome under their untrimmed beards. But they were the sort who had escaped civilization and were deaf to its requirements.

Hong Shou knew what to do to solve his problem. He wrote a letter and sent it with the next mail courier. Then he set up another caldron beside the first one. He made sure he had enough wood for the fires to boil the water. He strung up even more rope for drying clothes, and he got ready a large supply of soap. After that, he waited.

In truth, no one had ever taken much notice of Hong Shou until the day it happened, and then everyone did. Both his pots were full and all his lines were crowded. Hong Shou beamed as he washed the shirts and dungarees — and the long johns — and hung them up to dry.

A wagonload of young women from the city had come into the town. Each had a trunk of her possessions and each carried in her hand a copy of the newspaper announcement Hong Shou had sent off. The announcement said that rich gold miners were looking for wives and it promised that the first ones to arrive would have the best chance of finding a husband.

When their wagon pulled into town, there seemed to be miners everywhere. But by the time the young women unloaded their trunks, the town was deserted. However, since they had made such a long journey, they decided to sit upon their trunks and wait until these rich gold miners came to choose them as their wives.

By and by, the gold miners appeared. They were much changed. Their clothes were clean and even their beards were trimmed, for Hong Shou had also sharpened a pair of scissors. His gold mine had finally panned out.

♪

'Long the Way

Evil sniggers at courtship and love. Love is a calling.

    Strange, it seems, to many men for boys to dream of love since symbol of a manly man's a rooster, not a dove. When stricken with such amorousness, the young prince drew long frowns from courtly jesters saying that love's a weight that pulls one down.
    So he would ride each waking dawn throughout the countryside upon his steed, La Troubadour, and to the fields confide his inmost yearnings for a bride with whom to share his heart. Then looking to the sky he cried, "Oh, when will loving start!" He'd given up when a Hawk did glide behind La Troubadour and whispered something in his ear, then quick to heaven soared.
    The prince pulled reins and turned about — his answer was now known! He sped back to his castle home and ceased all lovelorn moans.
    He studied and he worked and grew into a kingly man; with virtue and strong points of view, he learned to take a stand. With goodness fed by honesty, he ever worked to build a kingdom of integrity through insight-driven skill.
    His thoughts of love were not forgot, in fact, they drove him on to build this kingdom free and just which common folk could join. 'Twas in the process of such work the young king met a maid who worked so selfless in the cause, refusing to be paid.

Their courtship lasted three sweet years, and then at last they wed. They lived a long and happy life just as the Hawk had said: "You'll find true love if what you love is goodness more than gain; so work for mercy and you'll find your true love 'long the way."

The Samovar

Evil says, "You need more." Love is content.

Nina tugged the heavy cart up the hill. She still had so far to go to reach the train. It would be a relief to let the train carry her load awhile. But it would only be a brief respite. She would have to pull it again the rest of the way to where the ship docked.

Nina was leaving her childhood home. Not many thought it was a good idea, but no one stood in her way. They thought she was foolish for going to that far away land to seek her destiny and didn't hesitate to offer loads of "expert" advice and cautions, as if they had previously made the same choice and the same trip, which of course they hadn't.

The heavy cart reminded her of her choice to leave as well as her choice of what to bring. She had envisioned herself starting out with only her shawl as protection against the elements and a small satchel in one hand to hold her favorite belonging. In her other hand she had wanted to carry a bunch of violets tied with a ribbon. It had been her desire to look just the way she felt about leaving to seek her fortune in a faraway land. But she had had too much company when it was time to pack up.

She had used some of the things after spending only one night along the way, and by far, she was the most comfortable of the other travelers who were heading in her same direction. But the rest packed up much more quickly in the morning and were already far up the road. As she drew the cart after her up the hill, she wondered why none had stayed behind to give her a hand since they each enjoyed the food made in her cast-iron oven the night before and had each made use of her mirror that morning.

She didn't wonder why each had looked into the mirror and chuckled. The mirror was the most ludicrous item in her cart. She was just waiting to find a place to leave it beside the road but had to be careful. Her aunt would be appalled. It had been a birthday gift. Her aunt was of the mind, and frequently declared, "No woman has a chance in this world if she can't be sure she is immaculately dressed, with every hair in place."

Nina herself had wanted to chuckle at her aunt's emphasis on outward appearance over inward character, but under her aunt's eye she had reverently placed the mirror in the cart. She was sure there were mirrors in the place where she was going which would serve as well, even if they had less gilding on the carved wood frame. But Nina reasoned to herself, after the tremendous weight of the cast-iron oven, not to mention a chair, a sewing machine, and all manner of household paraphernalia, the opulence and weight of the mirror wouldn't add significantly to her burden. The only comfort Nina could summon as she felt the weight of her possessions was that, in the new land, all these things would probably turn out to be just what she needed.

Once on the train with the iron wheels and steam engine finally bearing the cart's load, Nina rested. As the other travelers spoke enthusiastically about what awaited them on the other side of the sea voyage, Nina realized that everyone on the train had a particular idea about what would make them a success. One had an invention that he carried in a specially made box (which never left his sight) that was going to procure his fortune. Another had a small vile of liquid (the recipe for which he had sewn into the lining of his vest) which was supposedly a miracle ointment with the potential to heal and promote growth.

A few others had carts laden with goods, but different from Nina's. One was filled with seeds and tools for planting a field.

That traveler couldn't risk not finding the means of his livelihood in the new land. Another cart was piled with books to sell which were banned in the old land but not in the new.

Still, no one had the variety of belongings that Nina had. All she could think of as the train methodically carried her onward was how she would lighten her load when the train journey came to an end. She could hear her father saying, "Only a barbarian would not sit in a chair. You'll need a strong chair that will make the trip. Take my favorite one." Nina had felt foolish on that first night of the journey, being the only one sitting on a chair while the other travelers had to make do with the ground. Likewise, her grandmother's cast-iron oven had been pressed on her with sentimentality. It was the heaviest item. Her father had also said, "My sainted mother, your dear departed grandmother, had the same wish to travel as you do. You can take part of her with you by taking her oven. She would like that." The quilt would also have to go — the one her mother's friends had made. It was not only gaudy but bulky, warm enough for a Siberian winter, but Nina was traveling in the summer. Her mother's friends had each embroidered a farewell message in a different square. The most perplexing message read, "We will always remember you as you were."

When the train stopped and she left the terminal, Nina unloaded these four bulky possessions from her cart — the mirror, the chair, the cast-iron oven, and the quilt — and bit her lip as the tears stung her eyes. She wished that they weren't so heavy because she knew that later she might wish she had them. But if she missed the ship for pulling a heavy load, she would have been better off to stay on the family homestead just as everyone had admonished. She turned from the busy street into a dark alley. All she could hope was that no one would ever find out that she had shed family heirlooms on a strange street in an unfamiliar town.

Nina did, however, keep the sewing machine. Her mother had always held, "A woman needs to have her own means of employment, and with a sewing machine, she is always guaranteed a job." In truth, Nina could sew without it. But her mother, when it was placed on the cart, said, "There will be value in speed when you are starting at the bottom. And you have already made so many lovely things on this faithful machine." Nina was fond of the machine.

When Nina heaved her cart in sight of the dock, she was curious to notice empty carts — abandoned, it appeared — as well as frantic bartering going on between travelers and locals. Nina found out soon enough that each person would only be admitted onto the ship with a hand-carried parcel, and that the scavengers who descend each time a ship sails will pay next to nothing for the possessions they know the ship line never allows. Space was at a premium and passengers either had to agree to the limits or give up sailing with the ship. But Nina wanted nothing to do with selling her possessions to opportunists.

She pushed her cart away from the crowd to decide what to keep. The sewing machine obviously had to be given up. She also left the broom. Now that she looked at it and saw it in light of the space limits, she wondered how she could have ever agreed to bring it. But her sister had held it out on the day Nina loaded the wagon and said, "I never feel like my house is clean unless I have been able to sweep. I painted the handle of this broom in your favorite colors." So Nina was obliged to put it in the cart.

Her former teacher had dropped something by on the same day saying, "If you have to be a foreigner, you'll want to be clean, and if they don't appreciate cleanliness over there, then you might as well come back to us." The washboard had seemed a valuable asset, but now it and the tub would have to be left.

Nina took only a cup and a bowl from the set of dishware that her mother had given. It pained her to leave all but two pieces behind, especially since her mother had said, "I won't be able to be there when you get married, but this is what I would give you. A nice set of dishware can turn a simple meal of poor newlyweds into a feast." Marriage was a far-off thought to Nina and she was curious that her mother was thinking of it. However, the dishes would break if they weren't carried in the wooden crate padded with straw. She wasn't strong enough to carry them that way. She knew they must be left.

That only left Nina with an armful of things that she bundled into her shawl, securely tying the corners into a single knot. She noticed that some people had given up taking the ship in order to keep their cartloads of things. They were turning around and heading back to where they had come from. Nina wondered if some of them would add to their carts from what she had left. She tried not to look because she knew it would be heart wrenching to see the person who claimed her sewing machine.

The ship was indeed full. The trip that ensued was taxing as everyone made do with what they had and tried to protect their meager belongings from theft. On top of this, all were impatient to be done with the journey. Every occupant of the ship was consumed with thoughts of how to approach the new land and some could talk of nothing else, to the chagrin of those who had to listen. Others refused to talk at all, knowing their ideas could be stolen just as possessions could.

When the time for the first meal upon the ship came, Nina pulled a samovar out of her bundle and began to heat water for tea. Many had gone without a warm drink for the length of their trip, subsisting on cold food and plain water, so the look and sound of the samovar steaming and hissing made the travelers draw in close. Nina was praised for possessing such an enviable apparatus. Not only was it tastefully painted in an old-fashioned style, but the whole presence of it conjured up memories of home and security. One passenger asked if he could buy the samovar from Nina. Having left his behind, he didn't realize how much it would mean to him to see one again, and seeing it now, he couldn't quite imagine going on without one. Nina declined politely, and when the price was raised, she declined even more politely. For the samovar had been the only thing Nina intended to bring with her from the beginning, and it was priceless to her.

During the lull of the voyage, Nina dutifully took out the thick volume that had been pressed upon her by her mother's mother when she was loading her wagon. Her grandmother had said, "Come what may, don't lose this one! For sure, you won't be interested in such a book until much later, but a time will come when you will need to be reminded about your heritage. Besides, it's light and easy to carry." She read it now, tracing the generations that made up her mother's side of the family, trying to imagine what all the various branches on the family tree would think of her going off and leaving the home place. They were all listed along with their various qualities and accomplishments, but Nina found she was most interested in the ones who were most briefly mentioned, for it seemed there was little good that could be said of them. Nina wondered. Then she had a flash of fear over how she would be written up in the next volume. If it became known that she left gifts from family along the way, she imagined her paragraph would be even smaller than the small ones.

With no expensive berth to retreat to, Nina sat unsheltered on the ship's poop deck and her thoughts drifted beyond the frothy wake back to the day when her cart was loaded. She hadn't understood why all of her family took particular notice of the samovar and derided her for putting it in. Her reasons for loving it had seemed to fall on deaf ears. Her aunt stated quite authoritatively that samovars certainly weren't used over there and burning coal in such a way was most likely even against the law. Her sister turned up her nose at the way a samovar produces soot and dirty ashes which have to be cleaned. Her mother suggested she would only attract Old World men with such an Old World method of making tea. Her father said that he certainly wouldn't want to add such a worthless item to a cart that was already so heavy.

In the chill salt air Nina was glad for the warmth of the samovar, as were others. Conversations and arguments were left off and even the tight-lipped ones drew in for a cup of tea when the steam began to hiss. The only times Nina questioned if she had done right to bring the samovar were when people offered to buy it and persisted until she was exasperated. But when they finally gave up, the solace of the steaming samovar gently and softly returned.

When the ship was moored in the new land, once again everyone became as strangers. Leaving the ship, Nina found herself confronted with confusion and unexpected difficulties in looking for work and a place to live. The modest amount of currency that she carried in her pocket surely had seemed a large sum in her old land, but here it was barely enough for a week of bread. And there were already many more just like herself wandering around willing to do the most menial labor for the most meager of sums.

After she had been days without any prospective work or lodging, she decided that perhaps now was the time her grandmother had foreseen. Possibly the book of her ancestors would hold the key to solve her dilemma of being homeless and destitute in this new world. Just as she flipped it open, a policeman took notice of her and hustled her from the bench which she had made home. As she scurried to collect together her belongings, the book inadvertently got left behind, never to be seen again.

She wandered the streets alone. There was plenty of time to wonder if her lack of success had anything to do with her discarded possessions. She considered the mirror and whether it was her unkempt appearance that kept her from being hired. She wondered if a landlord would look differently at her if he knew she possessed a few things to set up housekeeping, such as a cast-iron oven and her father's favorite chair. Perhaps with her own sewing machine she could have gotten hired on at the sewing factory that claimed to have no more machines available. She gave herself a few laughs imagining how ridiculous she would look carrying around a washboard and a broom with a painted handle or wrapped in a quilt telling her how much she was missed by women far away.

To Nina, even the items she now carried in her shawl seemed ridiculous. There was nothing to carve with the knife, nothing to cook in the pot, and nothing to eat out of the bowl. Only the samovar and the cup were used, but her bits of coal were running out as well as her tealeaves. The weather turned cool and she needed to wear her shawl instead of using it as a pack, so she decided to relinquish the pot, the knife, and the bowl.

Despair was leading to desperation as she saw neither a way to go forward nor a way to go backward. She couldn't think of anything to give her hope. Thus, she prepared her samovar to boil one last cup of hot water with the last of her coal, making a cup of tea with her last tealeaves.

At the very time Nina came to this moment of hopelessness, a well-to-do but forlorn widower had a dream. His wife had died a year before, leaving him with three small children. Although he had hired nanny after nanny for their care, they pined away for their deceased mother and no one could bring them comfort. Their sadness turned into various illnesses that lingered and worsened. The widower was beside himself. He had no one who could help him, and not even his money could purchase relief. His children were dearer to him than his own life, and therefore, it is not surprising that it was in the nursery — where he had fallen to sleep with all three leaning against him — that he had the dream.

The dream was simple but fantastic. The widower awoke with the images of the dream clearly before him, but he wondered if the dream was to be trusted as guidance or if it was indeed a trick of his own troubled mind. While his children slept and would be unaware of his absence, he left his home guarded by the butler and headed for a park to walk and clear his mind.

As he solemnly walked the sidewalk and turned the corner into the park, he let out a gasp. There before him was a woman seated beside a steaming samovar. She lurched off the bench, supposing he was a policeman coming to evict her from her temporary home, and in her fright, she dropped her teacup to the ground. The widower caught his breath. He apologized for startling her and asked her why she was sitting in the park so late at night, and especially, what she was doing with that contraption.

Nina at first expected that he too would want to buy her treasured samovar, so she began telling him that it wasn't for sale, particularly as it was her only possession now that the teacup lay shattered at her feet. She briefly recounted her trip over the water from her homeland where her many other belongings were left along the way, and how, even without a job or a place to live, she still dreamed of finding her way in this new land.

The widower, upon hearing the word dream, felt he should confess why he was in the park at such an ungentlemanly hour and why he had been so astonished to see Nina in the park. Nina listened in awe as he told his own story of despair and hopelessness, and how just moments before while he had been sleeping he had seen a vision of his deceased wife come into the nursery and touch the forehead of each of his three sleeping but ailing children. In the dream his wife had told him there was only one woman who his children would accept as a nanny. He would know that he had found her when he found a woman who owned nothing in the world except for a samovar.

Nina laughed when he said he had to consult a dictionary to find out what a samovar was, admitting that he at first thought it was a long-handled knife. When he discovered that it was an urn for boiling water used mainly by Russians with a cylinder in the center for burning charcoal, a chimney for letting off the smoke, and a spigot for serving the water, he confessed that he was sure the dream was not possibly trustworthy. Then came the moment when he turned the corner in the park and saw Nina.

The widower asked Nina to be a nanny for his children. Convinced by his sincerity and intrigued by the dream, she accepted the job.

After a year, when the health and happiness of the children had been restored, Nina and the widower were married. She came down the aisle that day holding violets tied with a ribbon and wearing a gown she had sewn by hand. In their home, the samovar was kept in a prominent place. She had been quite right. It was the only thing she had really needed.

♪

Yeast or Baking Powder?

Evil ignores facts. Love embraces facts.

Betty Jean and Betty Lou scarcely know now what to do to stop the leaven in their bread from rising up above their heads! It's growing high and wide and deep — now it's oozing 'round their feet! They try to run and cry for help, but ev'n 'fore they'd yelled or yelped, the dough had bubbled, covering them — trapping all their cries within.

But still, the oven can be used! They light its flame and watch amused as heat from opened oven door bakes the bread from roof to floor. But the air — too hot and dry — made the pair of Bettys die. In the days and weeks to follow many folk came to that hollow where the House of Gingerbread had been baked just as I've said.

Poor Betty Jean and Betty Lou, Betty Crocker cries for you! If you'd read that gingerbread's baked with powder, you'd not be dead. The moral is not hard to see: "Carefully read each recipe!!" But if you don't, then please don't wail if you end up inside our tale.

The Magic Chalk

Evil takes the easy way. Love is ready to rescue.

Gus was a small-time thief. He didn't actually need to steal and burgle to live, but he loved the feeling of slipping around unnoticed while the rest of the world slept. Taking a few things here and there just gave him something to show for his stealth.

A day came when Gus had no challenges left. He had robbed street vendors of their produce, gentlemen of their wallets, houses of their silver tea services, banks of their currency, and children of their holiday candy. But he was bored with the small-time loot that he could snag and escape with unhindered by the law. He felt he wanted a big challenge.

His heroes were the big-time crooks whose names and pictures got put up in post offices. Gus adored the four words that captioned their mugs: Wanted Dead or Alive. But he lacked the type of ambition that the professional criminals had. Those thieves desired both the wealth and the danger that came with crime.

Poor Gus only wanted the privacy of being awake at night, and he really only wanted to be recognized for his ability to sneak around unseen and unheard while the rest of the world slept. So he must be forgiven for thinking that what he really wanted to do was rob and steal. And yet, that is what made him interested in the magic chalk.

Gus found the den of one of the first-class burglars and asked him to train him for a really big heist. Of course, the first-class burglar spotted Gus as the naïve soul that he was. He winked and told Gus, "I've got the perfect getaway plan for a major break-in when the police are surrounding and the guard dogs are growling. Listen, you can go for any loot — jewelry, art, or even gold — and then escape through the dragnet of a hundred coppers."

This hooked Gus like no other promise could. He could already picture his face framed on a poster with those enticing words beneath: Wanted Dead or Alive. The crafty crook interrupted Gus's dreaming by putting a cylindrical stick into his hand. It was only a thick piece of chalk, and it was no longer than his hand.

The professional told Gus that it looked like simple sidewalk chalk, but it was magic. All one had to do when surrounded by the police was to draw a circle or a square or even a triangle on a wall and step right through. The police would be dumbfounded to see the thief disappear right before their eyes.

Gus rightly asked if the professional had ever successfully used the chalk. The master of crime surrounded by his booty waved his hand casually around the room and claimed that he had no need for crime at the moment, and besides, the chalk had so recently been created that he hadn't actually used it yet. But (and here he leaned into Gus's face) he knew those who had, and they were now living in the Tropics sitting on top of ten times as much booty as he had. Then the crook cautioned that the chalk could work if, and only if, something highly valuable had been stolen and the thief was surrounded by cops.

With the chalk in his pocket, Gus began to plan his extraordinary crime. He walked the streets in the daytime considering each bank, each jewelry store, each museum. So far Gus hadn't doubted that the chalk would work. Professional criminals were his heroes, and he couldn't imagine that they would lie.

The magic chalk opened up new vistas for Gus. He no longer had to content himself with easy-to-open doors. He could consider breaking glass, exploding a small bomb to enter a bank vault, or setting off alarms around a masterpiece painting. Gus imagined that if he was going to step through a circle which he drew with the chalk, he wanted to be able to get through it swiftly and not have to maneuver a large picture frame or be held back by the weight of gold. So finally, Gus settled on stealing the famous 17th century Spanish diamond tiara displayed behind glass in an exclusive jewelry establishment. The alarms would ring when the glass case was broken, but this was just what was needed to bring out the police which was needed to make the chalk work.

Gus donned his nighttime stealthy-looking clothes. He made sure the five-inch piece of chalk was in his pocket. He took an ax for breaking the jewelry store's front window and the glass case. He added a cloth bag for dropping the diamond tiara into.

It took determination for Gus to make noise and hit the glass window, but he finally summoned it. The crash made him cringe. When an alarm started ringing, he knew he had to continue. His second swing knocked the top off the glass box and the diamond tiara was deftly lifted and dropped into the cloth bag. Then he waited for the police. Over the ringing and pulsing of the alarms, Gus finally heard sirens, and then his own pulse quickened and he prepared to run. He had already chosen the alley that he would run to — one with a dead end.

As soon as the police arrived, Gus took off running. He was so happy that they were following him that he wanted to stop to thank them, but he knew this might throw off his plan. So, he ran as fast as he could to the back wall of the alley and turned to face the police. They all slowed down seeing that they had the thief cornered. Most put their hands on their hips, and some twirled their billy clubs.

Then, with flair, Gus turned around and began a circle with the magic chalk. The circle almost complete, he turned to look at the police. They were clearly amused and a few laughed out loud. Gus finished the circle and took a deep breath. He lifted one foot and thrust it toward the circle. Now all the police were laughing. Then, with a sudden lurch, Gus was through the chalk-drawn circle, and the police were left dumbfounded trying to quickly stifle their last chuckle.

Poor Gus was led into a chamber with guards standing all around, and a dressed-up guy motioned for Gus to be brought forward. A chopping block stood in from of him. Suddenly Gus was hit from behind and knocked to the floor. Someone asked him if he didn't know how to kneel in front of royalty. While Gus's face was pressed to the cold stone, he felt the chalk in his hand and decided to see if it would still work. With more speed than he had used before, he drew a square of sorts around his body. Instantaneously, Gus dropped out of the chamber, just barely escaping his beheading.

With relief, Gus looked around in the new place he fell into. It was green and he could see the blue sky above. He had just stood up to determine exactly where he was when a troop of soldiers came double-timing by. If he had stayed kneeling in the grass, perhaps he might not have been spotted, but as it was, he was captured and led away. Whatever these Oriental soldiers were saying completely escaped Gus because he couldn't understand a word, but he quickly understood that they meant to execute him. They tied his hands behind his back and made him kneel on the side of a hill while they walked about fifty feet away and began to load their guns.

Again Gus panicked and wondered if the magic chalk could work on grass. He fell back against the hillside and drew an irregularly shaped hole since his hands were tied behind his back. Once again he fell through. It was a tight squeeze because the hole he drew was so small. Just as the Oriental soldiers arrived at the place where most of Gus had disappeared, he managed to pull his foot through, although his shoe was left in the hands of one of the green-uniformed soldiers.

This time, Gus lay perfectly still, deciding not to move until he could tell where he was and who might be after him. He felt himself on a hard surface, and then he felt his legs being stretched at the same time that his arms were being pulled in the opposite direction. Somewhere from outside of his sight someone was laughing cruelly and turning the mechanism that elongated him further. With horror, Gus surmised that he was on a rack and being forced to confess by torture, so he decided his only hope was in confessing since his hands weren't free. He cried out that he did it, and when he was removed from the rack, he fell and wobbled, and in a flash drew a shape on the wall.

Now, he found himself in a white windowless cubicle, but with alarm he saw all around him humanoids in space suits approaching him with a syringe filled with blue liquid. Gus checked to see if his hands were free and found that they were, although the chalk was floating around in the air. He had let go of it in his terror. Just before the syringe found his blood vessel, he caught the chalk and drew a shape in the air. To his utter gratefulness, the magic chalk worked on space air as well as hard surfaces. He floated quickly through the shape and completely avoided the prick of the needle.

Gus only had a moment to consider that he was growing weary of this journey with the magic chalk because he found himself walking the plank of a sailing ship — blindfolded. He could smell the seawater and hear the waves hitting the vessel far below. At the same time he felt how small the chalk had become in his hand. A saber was prodding him from behind. When the saber poked something in his pocket, Gus was suddenly yanked back off the plank, his blindfold torn off, and the cloth bag removed from his pocket. The diamond tiara!

The Captain of the royal Spanish galleon held up the treasure and all the Queen's Guard cheered. It had disappeared from the crown jewels just the day before but was now back safely in the hands of its rightful guardians. Poor Gus was on the plank again and made to walk out to the end without the benefit of the blindfold. He saw sharks not too far off. But with the small piece of chalk at the ready, Gus made the leap.

Amazingly, the magic chalk worked on water as well. This time Gus found himself back in his own house sitting at his table looking at the piece of chalk. The chalk was five inches long again. Gus rubbed his eyes and wondered if it had all been a dream. His breath was coming heavily, and he was in a dripping sweat. Dream or not, Gus decided not to have anything to do with crime again. He got up to throw the chalk away, and, as he did, he made the strangest wet footprints all across the floor, alternating shoe - sock - shoe - sock …

♪

BAREFOOT SANDY

Evil says, "You've lived in vain." Love remembers.

Oh, how Sandy loves to run — he's fastest in the town. And with a dozen races won, he's gaining wide renown. At Regionals he takes his mark: Ready, Set, and Go! He's out in front right from the start; he gives them quite a show. It is his day. He takes the gold! The cheering crowd goes wild! They marvel that he is so bold to run a barefoot mile.

But time goes on and Sandy grows both gray and slightly round. Yet, deep inside, still Sandy knows he's fastest in the town.

The crowd is gone that cheered him on, but still their cry he hears. And one thing keeps him living on as he is passed by years: it is the hope that yet one day he'll set the pace again and hear the crowd with gusto cry as he does run and win, "Ol' Sandy's fastest in the town! His is a matchless style! Forever he shall have renown, *That golden barefoot mile!"*

This is the hope that drives men on as they are passed by years — that someday all the town will pause and give them one last cheer.

The Runner's Folly

Evil adroitly manages ambition.
Love forgets not gratitude.

On two opposing hilltops two mansions stood. A road connected the two hilltops as if it had been built solely to connect the two mansions, and so it had. This road, joining the two mansions, was kept in excellent condition to fulfill an ancient agreement which bound them to equally share governance over the fertile valley that lay between them.

The populace of the fertile valley marveled at the ancient agreement, for it was apparent that they were treated more fairly and governed more equitably than other valleys. Each mansion, in the hope of winning allegiances and keeping peace, lavished gifts upon the farmers of the valley. Also, a grievance that did not receive a suitable hearing on one hilltop could be appealed to the opposing hilltop and the two mansions on the two hilltops usually found an agreeable solution.

The present generations that occupied the two mansions appeared to be remarkably good friends as well as complementary partners in governing. The road connecting the two mansions saw much traffic as daily social visits were exchanged and face-to-face governing sessions were conducted. On even numbered days the southern mansion hosted the northern mansion, and likewise, on odd numbered days the north hosted the south. The ladies dressed in lace and satin and the masters donned their best apparel. Beautiful horses were hitched to beautiful carriages to travel the road which twined through the valley. The winding distance was covered at a stately and regal pace in order to shower the valley farmers with blessings and gifts. Understandably, then, the farmers hurried to line the road each day when the gates of either one or the other of the mansions were flung open.

Coins, flowers, and sweets for the children were tossed from the carriages. With an eagle eye, each mansion watched as the carriage of the other mansion traversed the valley between the hilltops, taking careful account of the trinkets that were rained upon the awaiting valley. At the height of friendship and cooperation between the two mansions, the valley folk felt themselves to be blessed with security, understanding, and benefit. Surely, the ancient agreement linking the two mansions on the two hilltops was marvelous and earned the valley's full approval.

At this time Harry was but an athlete spending his days running through the hills, improving his speed, and making a reputation for himself as the running farm boy. Occasionally, he too would line the road and accept the free fall of coins and flowers and candy, but only if he happened to pass there on one of his runs.

He had already passed the age when a young man should decide how to make a living and give up play, but Harry's indulgent parents agreed to support him until he discovered a way to turn his running into an occupation. They had never heard of such a thing, but they adored their Harry and since they always lined the road at the coming out of the carriages and caught a pocketful of coins, they had no hardship in keeping him on room and board. Besides, they knew he had a good head on his shoulders and an ambitious spirit in his heart, so they trusted that he would find something.

It was on an even numbered day that Harry returned home from his morning run to find his parents in a gloomy state. They should have been enjoying their lunch and counting the coins they caught from the passing carriage which had emerged from the northern mansion's gates. The opening of the gates had regulated their lives as punctually as a clock. Just after daily lining the road, they always returned home to eat their noon meal. But today, the gates hadn't opened at the accustomed time, and when the time had well-passed that the gates should have disgorged the high stepping horses and glittering carriages, they dejectedly realized that they were not only hungry for their meal, but they also feared that something must be terribly wrong for the gates to stay shuttered.

Harry heard this news with none of the gloom of his parents. Like a good son with a good head on his shoulders, he promised his parents to find something out and come back with tidings, be they good or be they ill. But as no one in that valley could imagine what an ill tiding was, he only added that part with a wink to balance out his promise. As soon as he departed at a sprint toward the northern hilltop, his parents returned to their fields, but not without going around first to their neighbors to say that their Harry was going to find out why the big gates hadn't opened. For the rest of the afternoon they were heroes as various friends and neighbors stopped by to ask what they knew. They relished in retelling the story from the beginning to the end, and concluding with, "Our Harry will come back with tidings, be they good or be they ill," and just like Harry had done, they winked when they said "ill."

Harry used his run up the northern hill to think about what he knew regarding the two mansions. He knew that in each was a beautiful and queenly woman. They were similar in outside appearances, but his keen eye and ear had picked up that when one woman tossed out coins and candy and flowers, she didn't look at the people lining the road. The other one, however, looked out at the people and even greeted some of them individually and inquired after their health.

Some of the servants from each mansion were familiar to Harry. With each stride he remembered what he had heard from them. In the mansion on the northern hilltop, the servants performed their duties to a series of bells. At each sounding of the bells, one task should be completed and the other begun. In addition to these time-marking bells were other bells which either summoned a particular servant to the master's or lady's presence or summoned all the servants for special instructions. For instance, at the birth of the first child, all the servants had been summoned with this last type of bell and were given instructions to take individual cakes to each house in the valley to commemorate the birth. All in all, the bell system kept the northern mansion running smoothly, and none of the servants complained about the conditions, at least none that Harry had ever heard of.

Only one of the servants from the mansion on the southern hill was known to Harry — the stable manager. But from him, Harry had learned a very interesting bit of information: the master of the southern mansion was particular over the treatment of his horses. After the horses had performed a valuable service and exerted a great deal of energy, they were each groomed and fed and given the thoughtful kind of treatment that his servants were also given.

Harry was just about to reach the service gate of the northern mansion with the bells, thinking that he could claim friendship with several of the servants and thereby squeeze some information out of them, when it struck him that if the news was not good but ill, he would rather learn it from the mansion on the southern hill where the master was known to be conscientious about his horses. In a split second he judged that he might get a more sympathetic reception from the mansion where the master was concerned about those who served and exerted energy.

As Harry was turning on his heels and heading down the hill toward the southern mansion, he also realized that the lady who greeted the farmers by name as she threw out her coins and sweets was the wife of the master who was principled in the treatment of his horses.

With his strides falling into an easy cadence, Harry paced himself for the distance between the northern and southern mansions, clipping along the road as it wound through the valley. His presence did not go unnoticed. People in the fields called to him and waved as he flew by. But Harry was completely lost in thought, considering ways he might gain entrance to the mansion on the southern hilltop. It never occurred to him that his running ability was being marked by both mansions.

Going around to the side, Harry entered the rear courtyard. A handful of servants could be seen moving about their tasks — a gardener pushing his wheelbarrow of mulch to a row of shrubbery, a girl in a white apron and cap shining the windows on the outside of the kitchen, a young man with carpentry tools building a table — and then Harry spied his acquaintance in the stable. He sauntered over, not because he was winded, but because he wanted to act nonchalant.

"So, Paul, these horses haven't had their run yet today. I'll bet they're anxious to get harnessed and have their trot through the valley."

"Hey, Harry, what are you doing here? Did you get lost on your run? It's not their day to go out. It's the northern mansion that is supposed to be coming."

"Is that it? Well, I never keep track. It must be a lot of work for you when they come. When do you expect them?"

"To tell you the truth, Harry, I don't. There's something stirring, but I don't know what it is. The master came out once or twice looking like he was going to hitch up the carriage or just saddle one and ride over himself, but he never quite got to it. I've never seen him look so disturbed."

"As long as I'm here, Paul, let me give you a hand. You've got a lot of horses to feed. Does the master feed his servants as well as he feeds his ..."

"Young man! You there, ducking behind that horse. Come out, I want to speak to you. Were you the one I just watched run up the valley road?"

Harry showed himself from behind the horse and instantly sized up the mood of the master. He wasn't angry. He was troubled. The master indicated that Harry should follow. He led Harry inside through the kitchen (where Harry gave a nod to all the scullery maids and cooks) and down a long hallway, going past all kinds of rooms on either side, all of which Harry peeked into as he passed. And finally, the master of the mansion opened a door to a quiet study where two basset hounds slept near to the fireplace.

Conditioned by years of running over rugged ground and watching for pitfalls and small boulders that might trip him up, and at the same time carrying on in his mind a complex set of thoughts about how to make a living through running, not to mention thinking of more efficient ways his parents could run their small farm, Harry's mind was taking in all the details of the mansion he had just passed through as well as attending to the mood of the person he had followed and bracing himself for whatever might come next.

"I saw that you were helping my stable manager, Paul."

Here Harry was ready to defend a long and secure friendship with Paul, providing enough justification for visiting while Paul was at work, but he said instead, "Paul has told me how you care for your horses, Sir, and I was curious to see the animals up close, as I usually only see them in passing, and I adore horses myself, though you wouldn't know if from my occupation."

"Which is?" asked the master.

"I am at present an athlete and I'm thinking of training others to be athletes."

"Well, perhaps as you already have employment, you may not be available for the post I am looking to fill."

"Not at all," Harry interjected, realizing he had come close to missing an opportunity. "I am still in the initial stages and have not enrolled any students yet, so at the moment I am free to consider your post."

"Ah," the master sighed, "it's well that you are because your speed and your bearing make you the very person I am looking for."

At that first interview, Harry received the first message he was to carry to the northern mansion. It was simple enough to remember word for word, and yet Harry knew much had been left unsaid by the master of the southern mansion. The master tried to say that there was no alarm that the customary visit hadn't been paid, but then he had paused too long before finishing the message, looking sorrowfully out the window. Harry accurately surmised that something had gone awry at the last visit.

The conditions for Harry's employment were fixed. If he could carry messages word for word, repeat them in the hearing of the master of the other mansion, and return with a message from him — with all due speed — then he could have a salary as well as eat the noon meal with the other servants. Lodging was a problem since the servant quarters were full, but Harry was quick to assure his new employer that his dear parents would be sorry to see their only son sleeping under a different roof. So it happened on that day when Harry had merely set off to find out why the carriages hadn't rolled forth between the mansions that he was employed and could earn a living by his chosen occupation of running.

When Harry announced himself at the servant's door of the northern mansion, a series of bells sounded before he found himself admitted into a study similar to the one he had left. He faced the master of the mansion on the north hilltop who was more imposing in height and girth than the one who was now his employer. With all appropriate respect and poise, Harry gave off the message word for word. While a response was being construed, he was sent to sit in the kitchen to drink whatever would aid his return journey.

Upon calling him back, and before giving him the return message, the master of the northern mansion with the sounding bells remarked, "I happened to see you running today and I must tell you how impressed I am with your speed. You recall to me my younger self. I too was a passable athlete at one time, but of course, had to give it up in order to govern diligently."

Harry nodded and took the compliment with grace and seemed to agree that running should be given up for more important work, but inside he was thinking how he would never have to give up running now.

While Harry was running back to the southern mansion, he mused over the huge disagreement that had come about. The initial messages were too bland to yield much fodder for gossip; despite this, Harry decided that he wouldn't gossip the news even though the whole valley might expect him to. He liked standing in front of the masters of the mansions and did not want to sully his good standing by being a gossip.

That evening in his parents' farmhouse, Harry satisfied them with the tidings that all was well and that the mansions had merely decided to cut back on the daily use of the horses and carriages and preserve the strength of the ladies. No one thought to question this as all attention was quickly focused on Harry's new job as messenger.

Harry appeared for work every morning and greeted his bosom buddy Paul in the stables and waved an arm to the gardener and carpenter and tipped his cap to all the girls in the kitchen. He carried the messages back and forth with speed and accuracy, quite frequently making several trips in one day. The northern mansion continued to seat him in the kitchen and provide him with a refreshing drink while a response was contrived, and therefore, he was able to cultivate a network of acquaintances among the servants in that mansion as well.

Now one day it happened when he arrived at work, instead of finding the master in the study, he found the lady. He was still given a message to learn by memory, but with a special injunction to deliver that message to the lady of the northern mansion. This Harry did. Then he faithfully brought back the response from lady of the northern mansion to the lady of the southern mansion. When the return message caused her to look downcast, Harry offered as congenially as he could, that surely the lady of the northern mansion really missed her but was reluctant to express it in words that he — the messenger — would have to repeat. At this, the lady of the southern mansion brightened and asked him to go on. Encouraged by her sudden brightening of countenance, Harry elaborated on what he noticed about the lady of the north.

In response, Harry received a sudden outpouring of the lady's heart in regard to the relations as they now stood between the two mansions. He listened with dropped jaw as details came forth in deep sighs from the lady about just where the main grievance lay. But all at once, the lady of the southern mansion pulled herself up short for having been so open with a servant, begging him to understand that she had been overcome with sorrow and making him promise not to repeat any of it.

Harry willingly promised because he now saw for the first time the enviable position he was in. He alone, if he adroitly carried out his job, would be the only one in the valley to know all that there was to know about the relations between the two mansions. He was glad that he had decided not to gossip what he knew because that would eventually have come back to the ears of the masters and ladies, and then he would have quickly found himself as an unemployed runner. He also predicted that he could become much too invaluable to fire since he would know too much and perhaps he would know so much that he could begin to choose his own terms of employment.

In his time off, Harry jogged through the valley in close proximity to the farm plots because to him nothing felt better than for all hands to stop work and be raised in greeting. When he was asked what he knew, he gave half-answers and filled them with good tidings. He knew he was admired for his daily access to the mansions, but he planned to be admired even more when he was promoted to some sort of indispensable messenger, perhaps with younger runners to train in the art.

The next day when he appeared for his first message of the day, he ventured to tell the master of the southern mansion that when he had been at home in the evening, he noticed that there seemed to be some restlessness and unease due to the absence of the daily visits between the mansions. Without saying the people missed the coins and the sweets and the fragrance of the flowers, he said the people missed seeing the stately figures of the ladies and the majestic grace of the horses. When Harry bore the southern master's message verbatim to the master of the northern mansion, he added on the same observations about the people of the valley.

To Harry's delight, that very afternoon both mansions' gates were flung open and horses and carriages emerged. The flare and aplomb of the northern carriage as it wound its way through the valley was matched by the openness and dignity of the southern carriage. However, when they reached the halfway point along the meandering road where the regional road intersected it, one carriage turned off and followed it to the west and the other turned off to the east. From both carriages were flung coins, flowers, and sweets, while from only one carriage came also greetings and salutations.

For the next period of time, the messages that were sent back and forth between the southern hilltop and the northern hilltop were dedicated to the affairs of governing. It's true that in the beginning the messages had borne a more personal flavor and the southern mansion begged the northern for reconciliation. But even when such pleas seemed to fall upon deaf ears, the southern mansion continued in the silent hope of harmony being restored.

On a busy day Harry might make five or six trips between the two mansions conveying the various negotiating stances for a certain decision that needed to be reached. Both parties were stubborn along certain lines. For example, the master of the northern mansion insisted that all resources of the valley be used to make a profit and at the end of the year, if there had been a profit, the general populace could benefit by receiving an extra bonus, such as a goose for the holidays. However, the master of the southern mansion where Harry was employed insisted that the resources of the valley be used in such a way to enhance the lives of the people in the valley throughout the year including passing along regular bonuses.

So as Harry's legs and feet carried him along the road that connected the mansions, his mind worked back and forth between the two opposing positions regarding resources. Usually he would deliver his message word for word, and then bow his head a bit and say:

"But if you will not take it amiss, Sir, I might add that the master of the other mansion seemed to hesitate as he dictated that part of the message, and so perhaps he would be flexible upon that point."

These intrusions of Harry's were never taken amiss because he took the utmost care in judging the mood of each master before he spoke. And as he saw that there was a dearth of other counselors present, his third opinion was usually accepted. Occasionally, he also had great success offering the feelings of the general populace toward the problem at hand, and since he still lodged in his parents' farmhouse, he was considered a credible source of valley information.

Harry became quite comfortable in his role of messenger, counselor, and representative of the valley. The ladies of the mansions had nearly forgotten the way they used to visit daily, and the carriages, when they did go out, went in opposite directions. The masters of the mansions found that governing was somehow getting done, and so all discussion about returning to the former way of meeting face-to-face to fulfill the ancient agreement ceased.

Harry's dream of earning a living by running was accomplished, but Harry had been adding to that dream. Now he set his sights upon being named an under-governor. He felt he had discovered his talent for arbitrating and he longed to be recognized. He also had represented the valley to the two mansions and he desired to be credited for the resulting improvements. He especially thought he deserved such a promotion since he had never gossiped about the goings-on in the two mansions to the valley folk. Of course, he would take the liberty of passing on gossip between the servants of the two mansions. It seemed to please them greatly, and it assured him of a good welcome by both. He loved being admired by everyone he met and could only imagine how good it would feel for the admiration to grow.

Perhaps if he hadn't been desirous for more admiration, he might not have fallen into the trap. But as it was, he was impatient to advance in his position. The master of the northern mansion boldly let the hint drop one day that if Harry would work for him, his salary would be doubled in an instant and he would be lodged in a premium room with his own fireplace. Harry cared little for money and was content to live with his parents, but in his mind this offer sounded like the chance he was looking for to break out into the under-governor position he imagined.

Without much concern for the master of the southern mansion, he gave sudden notice that he was changing mansions, quoting higher salary and lodgings on the premises as his main reasons. If Harry had sincerely thanked the southern mansion's master for the fine working conditions and acknowledged how much he enjoyed his work, the southern master would not have suspected Harry of any wrongdoing. But, as Harry was leaving much unspoken about his own ambitions, he also left unspoken appropriate words of gratitude.

It had never occurred to Harry that he would be under the management of the bell system. Once lodged at the northern mansion, Harry first noticed how much less freedom there was to move about and gossip with the kitchen girls. Whereas he used to be seated in the kitchen for a refreshment, now he had to respond to a certain sequence of bells to call him out of his quarters to the study of the master. The master and lady of the northern mansion did not tolerate any servant who chose to ignore this very tried and true method of household management.

As well as moving according to the bells, he was no longer free to visit his parents daily in the valley and jog along the lanes and greet the neighbors and find out their hardships. The first time he tried to insert how the valley folk felt about a certain decision, the master of the northern mansion cut him off, reminding him that he no longer lived there and was not an expert any longer on the conditions and feelings of the valley.

To add to this surprise, Harry was rebuffed the first time he stood before his old employer at the southern mansion and tried to add his observations to the message. His old master immediately suspected him of conniving to alter the content and threatened to send back a message that he was interfering with the governance of the valley. This brought Harry to the full realization that he was now a simple, two-legged message boy, and that all avenues for assisting in the governing of the valley were closed to him. His old employer didn't trust him anymore, his new employer treated him like a piece of property, and he deplored his haste in bringing all this to pass.

Without his add-on arbitration, matters began to get worse between the two mansions. His hands were tied and only his feet and mouth were wanted to carry messages that often were met on both sides with explosions of anger. The quoted words became more and more acerbic as each mansion tried to force its way, and Harry had to be the one to repeat these words and receive the violence of the response. Too soon, Harry began to be associated with the messages themselves, and it deepened his growing sense of failure to be chastised for the words he only quoted.

He gave some thought to admitting to both mansions how he had operated before — adding information to their messages — and thought perhaps they would both desire peace enough to allow him to do it again. But he knew it wasn't a thing they would allow now that one mansion distrusted him and the other mansion owned him, even assigning a certain bell signal to his movements. He played out the possible array of messages it would take to convince both mansions that he should be allowed to take on the role he had before. It would be endless, and since he would be giving all the messages, his truthfulness would be suspect and all the words out of his mouth questioned. Furthermore, his new employer, he was sure, would not agree to any enhancements on any message, although without knowing it he had received them many a time. Besides, he would demand unwavering loyalty to his interests and not give a care to what was best for anyone else.

This current state of mistrust and of being owned was disquieting to Harry. He found that it acted as weights to his legs and a block to his mind. Unknown to himself, as he covered the distance between the two mansions, he was being clocked, and it was noted that he didn't run as fast as he used to, and it was also noted that his bearing as he stood and gave the messages was not what it used to be.

Harry returned to his quarters after delivering a particularly devastating message to his former employer at the southern mansion wherein the master of the northern mansion had declared the ancient agreement a roadblock to progress and a new mode of government was being put into effect. The master of the southern mansion had been too upset to dictate a return message and sent Harry off with a flustered hand. While Harry waited in his own room, sitting in front of his cold fireplace, he heard his individual bell sounding, so he went to stand before the master of the northern mansion without a return message to give. The master declared:

"I only agreed to take you on as a messenger on a trial basis, as I do all my servants. I am disappointed to say that your performance does not measure up to my standards. Besides, the absence of a response from my partner in governing must mean he concurs with my plan, or else you are still in league with him and are keeping something back. Well, whatever ..., I don't want to be a detective where matters of disloyalty will be exposed. I advise you to move back to your old master or return to farming."

In this way, the master of the northern mansion severed relations and communication with the southern mansion. Harry's place as runner was quickly filled by the master of the northern mansion. He recruited twenty runners, none as good as Harry but all able to repeat a simple message. He sent them throughout the valley to declare that he was now the sole governor.

Back on that first day when the carriages had not traveled the road, the master of the northern mansion had seen Harry almost enter his servant's entrance, and he had never forgotten the look of sudden calculation that had come across Harry's face. He had already decided that there would be no reconciliation with the southern mansion, but when Harry appeared later in the day with a message, he immediately saw how he could make use of such a runner who seemed to have a good head on his shoulders and an ambitious spirit in his heart.

All the while that Harry was carrying message after message between the mansions, the master of the northern mansion was putting the pieces in place for his complete takeover of the valley. While the master of the southern mansion was kept distracted by the false hope of restoring the ancient agreement, the northern master had been holding secret meetings with all the valley's key residents, promising them positions of influence in the new order. So, Harry never really had a chance to become an undergovernor after all; and from that point onward, he was never to find the same enjoyment in running as he had known before.

♪

TIGER, TIGER

(Revisiting W.M. Blake)

Evil calls destruction progress. Love sees through lies.
Jungle creatures round him cried as their keen eyes did him spy — this was not his habitat, Birds dropped doo-doo on his hat. Laughing Monkeys made him cry as his fist shook in the sky, "I am here to help your land! You don't seem to understand!"

Then a Toucan said curtly from the shadows of a tree, "I think, Mister, that you should leave our jungle, leave our wood. 'Tis your kind who robs from us that which God gave to our trust. When you're here then we're not free. Go back home and leave us be!"

Then cried man in full disgust, angry that they would not trust his intentions, pure and good, "God gave man your trees for wood!"

Yes, the Toucan saw through him ... knew the reason he came in — to their jungle, to their wood: he sought all the wealth he could.

Then a Tiger from the deep made him bleat like frightened sheep; turning tail and running 'way, vowing he'd be back some day.

Now that jungle is a farm with big tractors and big barns. Stopping progress, jungle tried; in the end they had to die. Now survives the strongest race — that's the one with human face — but the human heart is gone as the weak are trampled on.

Tiger, Tiger, burning bright
In the forests of the night,
Burning as the jungle creeps
Into mem'ry — all hearts weep.

The Kangaroo's Secret

Evil begins with a lie. Love liberates.

Little Pogo had just gotten big enough to leave her mother's pouch. Up until then, Pogo had only seen the world pass by as she peeped over the edge of it. Her mother had strong legs that could leap great bounds and even outrun a dingo; Pogo had heard the yap of the wild dog many a time but had always felt safe inside her mother's pouch.

Now that Pogo was too big for the pouch, she got to pull up grass and munch on leaves beside her mother. It took a lot of Pogo's little hops to equal one of her mother's hops, but she did her best to keep up.

As far as Pogo knew, they were the only two kangaroos in the whole world. Her mother told her so. It was impressed upon Pogo to always stay close because the wild dingoes wanted to wipe out the only two remaining kangaroos. Therefore, the dingoes were ever on Pogo's mind. She had nightmares about being eaten by them, especially as they had already eaten all the other kangaroos that had ever lived.

Pogo's mother, as you might guess, was being dishonest. There certainly were other kangaroos, but Pogo's mother didn't like to be around them. She had a variety of grievances against them and found it far easier to live in a secluded part of the bush where she never had to talk to them or even see them. And better yet, she never had to talk about them, either.

Since Pogo didn't know about other living kangaroos, she never of course asked to see any. But as any small kangaroo will, Pogo asked many questions, usually when her mouth was full of grass or when she was supposed to be going to sleep. She wondered where she came from and where her mother came from and whether a wild dingo had ever nearly killed her mother and is that what happened to her father and can't kangaroos fight against dingoes since they are so strong and are kangaroos strong and do they ever eat anything except grass and leaves?

Without any other living kangaroos around, one might think that Pogo's mother would have been tolerant of hearing and answering questions since there was no one else to talk to. But every question from Pogo threatened to reveal the secret Pogo's mother was guarding. It troubled Pogo's mother that the questions never ceased. She had never imagined that a small kangaroo could think up so many things to wonder about. Consequently, keeping a secret became so difficult. When Pogo's mother had left the other kangaroos to live privately and peacefully, she had only imagined that her offspring would be as content as she was to munch grass in solitude.

Pogo wondered about other things as well. She asked where the grass came from that they ate and why eucalyptus leaves taste as they do and where does the sun go at night and how does it get all the way around to the other side the next morning and have kangaroos always slept in the nighttime, like they do?

Here again, Pogo's mother was free to tell Pogo that all kangaroos sleep at night (when really they sleep during the day and eat at night). But with no other kangaroos around to disprove her, Pogo's mother gave a lot of good reasons to explain why kangaroos must sleep at night and eat during the day. The one reason that Pogo's mother left unsaid was that they slept during the night so that they couldn't possibly run into any other kangaroos, and, likewise, they ate during the day since all the other kangaroos were busy snoring and wouldn't see them.

All day long, Pogo slung questions at her mother. Innocent as she was, she never imagined that her mother had told her lies or that her constant barrage of questions made her mother weary. Finally, Pogo's mother decided that the only way out of the discomfort was to allow Pogo to graze on her own. But to do that presented other problems, such as wild dingoes or Pogo straying too far and seeing other kangaroos.

So her mother devised a plan. She told Pogo that all young kangaroos, when they reach a certain age, go out and gather enough leaves and grass to feed their mothers and fathers who are older and need to rest more. She told Pogo how fortunate she was to only have a mother to feed, and so therefore, would still have plenty of time to play. And then she told Pogo that whenever she heard her give a whistle, Pogo was supposed to return at once, and in a hurry, because it meant either danger or dinner time.

Pogo had a lot of questions to ask, but her mother pushed her out to begin her new job of gathering food. Before she had gone far, she heard the whistle and she hopped back with what she had gathered. This happened many times on the first day, as Pogo's mother had a very large appetite which had grown even bigger since she was sitting idle and thinking more. Poor Pogo was exhausted by the end of the day and went to sleep quickly without asking any questions. The plan worked.

The next day Pogo was sent out and told to gather grass, but more of it, and especially leaves from the acacia tree. Pogo gathered grass, and lots of it, but she forgot the leaves of the acacia tree. It's true she had gotten distracted by watching a beetle gathering his food, but also the acacia tree leaves were hard to reach, so Pogo put it off. The mother was now hungrier than ever and especially tired of just grass; but she didn't want to scold Pogo because scolding might thwart the way her plan was working. She knew how she herself would react if someone scolded her — she would stop working altogether and inform the scolder to do things for themselves. More than anything, she wanted to be free from answering Pogo's questions, so she had to keep Pogo happily gathering food on her own.

Therefore, she augmented her plan. She told Pogo that one whistle meant, "come home in a hurry," but a double whistle meant, "don't forget the acacia leaves." That way Pogo could gather grass and watch beetles and still remember to bring all of the right food. This new plan made Pogo feel more independent and thus, more happy.

After that whenever Pogo was out in the bush, she gathered grass, watched beetles, and listened for that special whistle. Sometimes it blew just when she was most interested in how a beetle was digging a hole, but Pogo always obeyed the whistle.

Very soon another whistle was added which meant, "bring a eucalyptus leaf." These were even harder to gather because the leaves were so tough to break off. Pogo had a very difficult time remembering to bring them, especially when there was a lizard to follow. Still, whenever the eucalyptus leaf whistle sounded, Pogo left what she was watching and gathered the aromatic leaf which her mother gobbled down greedily as soon as Pogo hopped with it into the nest.

For quite some time, life went on in this way for Pogo and her mother. Pogo's mother felt secure that her secrets were safe since Pogo was too tired to ask questions at bedtime and too hungry to ask questions while she ate. Pogo's mother was ever diligent to whistle for Pogo to return so that she could never venture too far away, thus keeping her from the danger of dingoes and from seeing other kangaroos. In fact, Pogo's mother was feeling extremely proud of herself and her system of whistles which kept her nicely fed, kept Pogo safe and happy, and kept questions to a minimum.

One day, which seemed like any other before it, brought a drastic change to the life of Pogo and her mother. Pogo was hopping around gathering leaves and grass, and Pogo's mother was reliving past grievances against other kangaroos (being glad she never had to see them again), when she heard Pogo yell. Immediately Pogo's mother whistled for her, but there was no swift return. She tried the whistle over and over and finally hopped out in time to see Pogo in a wooden cage being carried away on the back of a truck. In all of her protective scheming, she had never anticipated that humans would be a danger since in the area where she and Pogo lived humans were as rare as a dunny in the desert. She was incensed.

    She was still strong, although fatter than before, and with effort she kept within sight of the truck. After many many miles the truck stopped at a large tent. Pogo's mother was exhausted. There was a lot of activity around the tent. She saw many different kinds of animals being led around on ropes by people — monkeys, horses, an elephant, and even some fluffy dogs. It appeared to be an animal circus and she wondered what they wanted with her Pogo.

    It soon became evident. Pogo was let out of the cage by a man with a eucalyptus leaf in his hand. He held it out for her, but when she reached for it, he withheld it and put her back into the cage. Later in the day when her hunger had reached a peak, he returned. This time Pogo did everything she could to reach the leaf. After a particularly high hop, she was given the leaf to eat. In the days to follow this same thing was done over and over again by the man with the leaf and always when Pogo was very hungry. At each subsequent time, the leaf was given only after an even bigger stunt was performed.

    One day while Pogo was being trained, another trainer was working with the dogs. Whistles were being used to signal to the dogs to prance around the ring and perch on top of a ball. When Pogo heard the whistles, they sounded like those of her mother, and without being able to control herself, she began to make the motions of gathering grass and leaves. Her trainer was most amazed to witness this strange behavior in a wild kangaroo.

All at once, the trainer saw fantastic possibilities for a performing kangaroo who could answer to whistles. Instead of holding out eucalyptus leaves, the trainer began to use whistles. At length, Pogo became the wonder of the circus. No one had ever seen a kangaroo before who could be taught to perform according to whistles.

Pogo's mother watched in wonder as pictures of Pogo were put up on large signs and as hordes of people arrived from the nearby towns to watch Pogo perform. She once peeped into the circus tent while Pogo's act was on and stared in amazement at the stunts Pogo was doing. It made her angry to see Pogo humiliated by doing stunts on the back of a horse and tossing a ball with her tail so that slippery seals could catch it on their noses — all directed by some human with a whistle!

Word of a performing kangaroo traveled quickly, and kangaroos from everywhere were curious to see one of their own who had attained such fame. Some of the curious kangaroos recognized Pogo's mother. Without any malice they asked what she had been up to and where she had been. Then they suggested that she must be so proud of her daughter. In fact they assumed that she must have given her daughter to the circus to be trained.

Pogo's mother was now torn between the prospect of fame and the anger of losing her Pogo. But she couldn't allow it to be thought that she had given Pogo to the circus. She related the story over and over again to anyone who would listen about how Pogo had been stolen and how she was kept in a cage when she wasn't performing. She became most adamant when she pointed out that it was very unnatural for kangaroos to be kept in confinement and to be made to perform in the daytime when they should be sleeping and to be fed rather than being allowed to graze.

Someone finally asked Pogo's mother how it was that Pogo could do all those unusual stunts. Pogo's mother lividly blamed it on the trainer who mercilessly controlled Pogo with inhumane whistles. She assured everyone that Pogo was as normal a kangaroo as you could find and would never do those unnatural stunts except for the trainer and his whistles, avowing that she had never heard of a more shameful way of controlling someone than with whistles.

Once, when Pogo's mother managed to get close to Pogo's cage between training sessions, she had expected to find Pogo glad to see her and eager to get free. Therefore, it hurt Pogo's mother terribly to hear Pogo say that she enjoyed the circus and wanted to stay and that she didn't want to be turned lose. "Aren't you proud of me, Mummy?" Pogo asked. Her mother just smiled.

When she returned to the other kangaroos and reported that Pogo was very unhappy and being cruelly mistreated, she attributed many other words to Pogo that hadn't been said either but which were less embarrassing than saying the truth. These false reports inspired the kangaroo group to try bold tactics to free Pogo. They decided that, as a group, they could ravage the whole circus area and throw it into such confusion that Pogo's cage could be smashed and she could be freed.

Just before they could put their plan into motion, however, an accident occurred. Pogo was performing on a flying trapeze. Just when the whistle sounded for Pogo to let go and land in a net, raucous applause erupted from the spectators. Poor Pogo's timing was thrown off by the applause and she missed the net. Her fall onto the hard ground broke her back and she was dead.

When news of this reached Pogo's mother she acted sorely grieved. She spoke angrily about the circus men who had trapped Pogo and more angrily about the trainer for having brainwashed Pogo. And she claimed to even be angry at all the people who came out to watch Pogo perform and made her a famous kangaroo. Surely Pogo's mother was saddened, but tempering her grief was her relief that Pogo could never tell the other kangaroos how much she liked being in the circus. And mostly, she was glad that no one would ever find out the secret of the whistles.

Yet, unknown to Pogo's mother, another young kangaroo had visited Pogo's cage just before the fatal performance. He had wanted to become a circus kangaroo, too, and had asked Pogo how she had learned to perform. After Pogo got over the shock of seeing another kangaroo, she told him how her mother had trained her to answer to whistles while she was gathering food in the daytime. The boy kangaroo was amazed to hear about the strange life that Pogo had lived before she was trapped by the circus men.

Just as Pogo's mother was pretending to be grieved and angry, the boy kangaroo stepped forward with unusual courage and told everyone what Pogo had told him. When the other kangaroos heard everything, and especially about the whistles, they turned away one by one and left Pogo's mother quite alone as she had been before, though this time it wasn't by her own choice.

♪

THE SERPENT AND THE FOWL

Evil perverts truth. Love reveals truth.

Improbable as it may seem, a serpent gave birth to a fowl. Of course this was when impossible dreams on earth were still avowed.

And naturally it was the bird who counted herself as a snake, 'cos snakes all did know that such was absurd and played on her mistake. They exploited her eagle eye to warn of foes from the sky; subtly deceiving, they kept her believing that she could never fly.

Ironically, instincts would lead her up to the edge of a cliff, where heart fluttered free and she felt what could be outside the snakes' vile pit. But freedom aroused in her fear, "Snakes hearts are not meant to be free. Why, Mother would hiss such thoughts now to hear. This conflict must not be!"

Snakes' tether of praise from the pit recalled her service and wit; love-talk unleashing, subtly deceiving that she shall not be bit. But suddenly tether was snapped by eagle who swooped to her side! Snakes all aspersed that she was kidnapped and duped to be his bride.

Assuming all tethers were snapped, she flew as if totally free to love her new mate and chicks yet unhatched upon cliff's apogee.

Though their eggs had been laid far away, this scarcely could keep snakes at bay, 'cos as they were roosting, serpents were boasting, "We'll have those chicks someday!"

Still under the curse of snake lies, she watched her hungry chicks hatch; but seeing their food, she wanted to die instead of make the catch! They slithered up up to her nest. She knew their intent was her brood. Facing this truth — her ultimate test — her talons were fast unloosed!

Improbable as it may seem, a serpent gave birth to a fowl. Of course such a thing is no longer seen, well … at least it's not avowed.

The Pretty Peace Bird

Evil is vain.
Love is wise as a serpent and harmless as a dove.

Jonas was only a poor farmer, but he possessed a rare and unusual wisdom for one who knew he would only ever be a farmer. He and his wife joined their efforts and worked a very small farm. And since it was barely enough to support them, they both found other ways to earn money. Jonas's wife, Lottie, made quilts in the evening which she took once a year to the town and sold. During the winter Jonas carved wooden bowls and cups which he sold to traveling bands of Gypsies as they rolled by in their colorful wagons once each spring.

Jonas and Lottie had a son whom they named Solomon because they hoped that one day he could be just as full of knowledge and wisdom as the King Solomon was. Of course, Jonas could have used an extra hand on the farm and there were many ways a growing boy could have helped. But Jonas looked about the land in his small portion of the world and knew that he wanted his boy to go to school instead of being confined to working the land.

From the time that Solomon was born, Jonas and Lottie saved all the money they made from selling her quilts in town and his wooden bowls and cups to the Gypsies. Schools were rare in those days. They would have to send Solomon away to town and it would cost them.

The small family of three had no other goal than to send Solomon to school so that he could acquire knowledge and gain wisdom. Neither Jonas nor Lottie could read or write, but they helped Solomon learn the poems they had learned in their youth. Before Solomon was ready to go to school he could recite many stories this way.

The day finally came for young Solomon to go to school. Solomon was dressed in his best and the wagon was loaded for the trip. All three made the trip to the town, glowing with anticipation.

Jonas and Lottie were naturally in awe of the headmaster and the school and the trappings of education. They had no misgivings about turning their young son over to be taught since they were convinced they were doing the very best for their only son. On the much-anticipated, day Solomon was turned over to the headmaster along with full payment for the first term. He was assigned a bed and a stool and given his first book.

While they settled young Solomon in his new room, Jonas and Lottie were proud that their son was a student as well as proud that they, poor farmers, had saved their money to pay his way. None of their words captured just how proud they were. They beamed from ear to ear and continually patted Solomon on the back and on the head. Solomon was likewise proud that he was their son.

Thus, they parted, all of them happy and feeling content that a wonderful world was going to open up to Solomon from the inside of books and the heads of teachers.

Other boys came to the school. The room where Solomon had his bed was filled with boys and their noise. Needless to say, the first days were too exciting for expression. Solomon was readily accepted by the boys in his room who were also in his class, and he woke up each morning and went to bed each night in those first days feeling glad that there were other boys in the world. Solomon learned the boys' names and eagerly joined in their games.

The headmaster called Solomon to him one day to assess what he already knew. He asked Solomon if he could read or write. When Solomon answered that he couldn't do either but he could recite poems, the headmaster sniffed and said that was of no use. So Solomon was placed in the lowest seat of the class, but he didn't mind. As long as he was in school he couldn't be discouraged.

Unfortunately, Solomon was soon to learn that the headmaster was a man of unkind words and actions. Solomon put forth his best effort hour by hour to master the alphabet and their sounds and to join them into words with all the letters in the right order. By all accounts, Solomon was more willing to learn than the headmaster was willing for him to learn. Every success of Solomon's brought a reproof by the headmaster. If it hadn't been for the other boys, Solomon wouldn't have known that he was improving. Their amazement at his sudden progress in reading and writing was Solomon's only clue that he was learning.

No letters were written by Solomon to his parents because they couldn't read. However, the other boys wrote letters to their parents but had to have them censored before being sent out. The headmaster was strict about what kind of information left his school, and every letter had to cast him in a generous light. So it wasn't until the autumn holiday that Solomon was able to tell his parents anything about the school and show them that he could read and write.

Their little farmhouse was filled with the delights of seeing their son make letters that made words that made sentences. Solomon was begged to read over and over again whatever he wrote. Jonas and Lottie could barely contain their satisfaction that their own son was a student who could read and write. They never tired, as well, of hearing all the names of the boys Solomon knew and all the games they knew how to play. It was a happy holiday unmarred by any sadness.

Only on the last night did Solomon mention the unkindness of the headmaster. They had never known their son to lie or even tell a partial truth, so the news upset them greatly. On the one hand, there was no one more esteemed in their opinion than a school headmaster, but on the other hand their son had told them of some very dishonorable words and deeds.

Jonas and Lottie carried Solomon back to the school in the wagon and on the way, they encouraged him to learn all he could and do his best to withstand the ways of the headmaster.

When they arrived, the headmaster greeted them quite warmly and invited Jonas and Lottie in for a conference, which set them at ease and engendered hopeful smiles. Their faces, however, when they finished were unlike their faces when they had begun. Smiles and hopefulness had been replaced with drawn looks and disbelief. That their goal to see their son gain knowledge and wisdom could already be at an end was sad news indeed. The headmaster had told them that Solomon had no capacity to learn and was better suited to the farm, but he conceded to keep him on for a second term, especially when Jonas added an extra sum to the full payment.

New teachers had been added to the staff, and it was for this reason that the headmaster claimed to need more money. He told them it required more of everyone's effort to educate the boys whose parents didn't know how to read or write, adding that the new and very qualified teachers were already expressing dismay that their classes must also include children of deficient background. Is it fair to the advanced students to be held back by the slower ones? The headmaster said that he was sure Jonas and Lottie could empathize with the difficult position he was in. After all, all farmers know that yoking unequal oxen together makes for mighty crooked plowing.

The next term predictably brought out more of the headmaster's cruelty, not physically, but verbally. He was of the mind that if he never laid a hand on the boys he was beyond all criticism, and he continued to edit each letter that was sent out to the parents. The teachers who had been added were cut from the same cloth as the headmaster. They each made it their goal to disparage the students in various ways, whether in setting some of the boys up as model students who dare not fail, or others as dunces who dare not succeed. Solomon was always in the second group.

During the spring holiday break, Solomon once again demonstrated for Jonas and Lottie his newly gained knowledge and he once again revealed the treacherous ways of the headmaster and the new teachers. According to Solomon, many of the boys tried to tell their parents, but the parents accused the boys of being liars and beat them for saying a word against the revered headmaster and the very qualified teachers. Then Solomon suggested that he had had enough of education and he would rather stay home on the farm where the headmaster said he belonged. This note of resignation gravely alarmed Jonas, and he then knew that something had to be done. He didn't know what, but he convinced Solomon to give it another try.

It was spring and time for the Gypsy caravan to pass through. Before taking Solomon back to school, Jonas' bowls and cups had to be sold.

Over the years Jonas had become friends with one particular clan among the Gypsies. After he had bargained and sold most of his wares, he visited their colorful abode for their annual cup of tea and honey. As they recounted the highlights of the past year, the situation at Solomon's school was related to the Gypsies. Now the Gypsies had never encountered a school or a schoolmaster for that matter, but they were nonetheless expert in reading people. They said they knew just the thing to do. The school needed their Pretty Peace Bird. In such a situation the bird could work a magic that would allow the students to study in peace. But it would take some time and patience.

And thus it was that accompanying Jonas and Lottie and Solomon in the wagon on the return to the school was a yellow bird in a cage. It looked like an ordinary bird that could please the ear with a song, but as we know, it had another ability as well.

Only Jonas knew of the bird's magic. Solomon was prevented from knowing so that he would not be able to inadvertently spoil its secret. In fact, only Jonas could make use of the bird's special ability. No one else would be able to tell that it was anything other than a yellow songbird that was content to swing in a cage.

Had the headmaster not been so interested in free gifts that he could freely manipulate, the bird might not have hung from a hook in the front of the schoolroom for the remainder of the year. But he could see no danger in receiving a free gift from a country bumpkin like Jonas.

So, there it hung. Its little black eyes darted to and fro and it hopped from rung to rung. Even the teachers were pleased with the caged bird, mostly because it gave them one more area to manage the students. Each boy was assigned to feed the bird and clean the cage in turn, and the headmaster and teachers used the boys' efforts either to praise the ones who couldn't fail or chastise the ones who couldn't succeed.

At the end of the school year, Jonas came early to town in his wagon. As he took Lottie around to sell her quilts, he invited everyone they met to come to the school's end-of-the-year-program to see his magic bird. There was much interest in a magic bird and even the mayor of the town heard about it and decided to come.

The school hall was crowded with the students and their parents and the town's people for the closing assembly. Jonas had never seen so many people gathered together in one spot before and he didn't relish the idea of standing up in front of them. He almost gave up his idea. But the bird in the cage seemed the only way to secure his Solomon's way toward gaining knowledge and wisdom. With this thought he plucked up his courage.

Just after the headmaster had bestowed awards on all the students who could not fail and after he said many other false things about the pleasure it was to teach all the boys, Jonas made his way to the platform with the bird in the cage.

The assemblage hushed all noise at his boldness. "Our boys need to be allowed to study in peace," Jonas said. He then held up the bird in the cage and he spoke these seven words: "Pretty Peace Bird, Say what you heard." At those seven simple words (which only Jonas knew to say) the bird began to repeat everything it had heard the teachers say in the classroom where it had hung, and more than that, it perfectly imitated the voice of the one who had spoken. Granted, everyone would have had to listen a long time to hear everything, but merely a few minutes were enough. The headmaster reached out his hands as if to stifle the bird and the teachers started up out of their chairs, but Jonas stood his ground and held the bird out of their reach.

The town's people listened aghast and the parents suddenly realized that their sons hadn't been liars. The mayor was the one who summed up everyone's reaction. He removed the headmaster and the teachers from their jobs.

Immediately, the town's people rose and requested that the Peace Bird be hung permanently in the schoolhouse to ensure that the students could study and learn in peace unhindered by unkind words or deeds again. The mayor agreed and was just reaching for the bird when Jonas held it aloft and out of reach again.

"No," he said, "this bird, although pretty, is dangerous. We must learn from our experience rather than depend upon the bird to make peace for our children."

Just as it had been agreed upon in the beginning, Jonas set free the Pretty Peace Bird to fly back to the Gypsies.

In time, Solomon finished school and gained knowledge and wisdom. Jonas and Lottie were proud, so proud, in fact, that they had no words to express it. And Solomon was proud that he was their son.

♪

Ms. Tack is Back

Evil controls. Love frees.

The principal, standing in front of us all, cleared her throat and then seemed to grow tall: "Good evening, dear parents, my name is Ms. Tack. How pleased I am to welcome you back. Seems only like yesterday that you were here and ... Oh my! Jimmy Jones, you're still in the rear?" The parents all chuckled, except Jimmy Jones. (Today he's a builder who's built his own home.)

Ms. Tack then smiled the smile children all fear: "Dear parents and guardians, do lend me your ear. So much has changed since you filled up these chairs that it is my duty to make you aware of rules — Golden Rules — which now govern this school. In fact, all the rules are but learning's new tools to guide all the children so none seems a fool. Rule Number One is ..." and Ms. Tack went on, expounding the Rule Tools that learning builds on, guiding all minds on ascent to the thought that School Rules are basic to each subject taught. (But Jimmy, the builder, did wonder how *rule* is somehow a synonym for the word *tool*. Because, in his job, tools should never be laid inside the foundation as structure is made.)

"... Rule Number Thirty-Three's last but not least: it's fundamental to each other piece! Our school is not here for the children alone — we need as a supplement each of your homes. So, as you do exit, my aide, Mr. Bruce, will give you a packet to carefully peruse that helps you to build up a home where your child can learn and succeed and grow bright and be mild. Our Motto is printed on top of each page: 'Schooling's not done, no matter the age!'

"Please, do sign the Contract. Return it this week to show that our rules you will day-by-day keep. Yes, school is not here for your children alone — our school is a model for each of your homes."

Just then, a huge time machine dropped in the hall, and Ms. Tack, inside it, was no longer tall. And Jimmy Jones peeked from around the machine; he looked at the crowd and said, "I'd better come clean that on my free weekends I work in my shop, creating machines which can make time flip-flop. I went home last week and I thought of Ms. Tack, and thought that it might help if she would go back. She says that success is to know the school rules. Ms. Tack, please forgive me, but that just ain't school! Now, go back. Discover! Such rules aren't the aim — learning the subject's the name of the game. So parents and guardians who lent her your ears, fear not to stand up when Ms. Tack reappears."

Ah … such is the stuff fairy tales are made of, 'cos Ms. Tack is back and she's got boxin' gloves.

The Bridge

Evil makes reality hard to see. Love sees it.

A bridge spanned a turbulent river. It was a stone bridge that had been made before memory. Some said it had been made by their own ancestors who used it to expand their domain in wars against other tribes. Others said it had been made by conquering tribes who had invaded them. At times it had been a fiercely contested bridge and the sight of gruesome slayings, but that was all in distant history. It was now just the bridge that connected the two sides of the river where Samuel lived on one side and Sarah the other.

The river itself was impossible to cross except for the bridge. The swift current and submerged rocks made any attempt in a boat dangerous and fatal. Even the bridge seemed to arch high out of fear of the river. However, when the churning and swirling water swelled after a heavy rain, it never rose as high as the bridge. Therefore, the bridge was never washed away.

Samuel and Sarah crossed the bridge every day to see each other. They gave little thought to the rocks and current below because the bridge was so strong that not even a fierce wind could shake it. They thought the bridge would stand forever. When it became their plan to marry, they decided that Sarah would join Samuel on his side of the river. Sarah's people warned her against crossing the river to live, but she assumed that they were merely afraid of what they didn't know.

One night while everyone slept, a sorcerer (who holds quite a different job by day) crept around the bridge on the side that Sarah lived on. He raised his arms and spun around and shouted out some vile sounding words, and all at once, the bridge vanished. The next morning, the town people gathered at the water's edge, troubled by the disappearance of the bridge. They felt that it was a warning for Sarah who was thinking of crossing it — not for commerce or necessity — but to live on the other side. Since she was the first in many generations to have made such a plan, the town people shook their heads from side to side, declaring that this is what happens when young people with fool-headed ideas ignore sound advice.

The people dispersed from where they had gathered, leaving only Sarah looking across the raging waters to where Samuel stood. Till then, neither had really noticed just how swift the current was. Each tried to speak to the other, but the rush of the river drowned out their voices. They tried hand signals but had no way to give meaning to their motions. In frustration, they waved as meaningfully as they could and turned to go to their own work.

Sarah's parents pretended to sympathize with her as she pined for Samuel. In actuality, it was they who had called upon the sorcerer to find a way to prevent the union. They were embarrassed that their own daughter would join the other side. Samuel's parents, on the other hand, truly did sympathize with him. In his desperation to get across, his father and brothers tried to help him navigate the river in a boat. But the boat quickly capsized, and they all swam back to shore, barely saving their lives.

Daily, Samuel and Sarah stood on the opposite banks, waving to each other, trying to express unrelenting love in each wave of their hands. The people on Sarah's side called her wicked for bringing this catastrophe upon them and held her responsible for their loss of business with the other side of the river. Poor Sarah was harassed by them day upon day.

Sarah's parents implored her to give up her ideas about marrying Samuel and to consider the offers of the young men on her own side of the river. The daily scourges of the town people and her parents' appeals were wearing her down. Her youthful face grew lined and drawn, and her once ready smile was only present when she stood on the banks of the river and looked across at Samuel. Her parents kept insisting that she marry one of the young men on her side (and they had one in mind), because if she did, the bridge would surely reappear and the town people would stop assailing her and her family.

In the meantime, Samuel was not idle. He was always thinking of a way to get across the river. He knew that with time he would find a way. Then one morning while Sarah was waving to him and he was trying to make out if she was smiling or crying, a stern-looking man came up to her and said something that made her turn away. Although Samuel couldn't hear what was said, he could make out by the slump of her shoulders that Sarah's will was being worn down, and Samuel didn't like the way the man had taken a hold of her arm and moved her away from the shore.

That vision troubled Samuel all day and all night. He forgot his work and he couldn't eat and he couldn't sleep. He deplored his lack of knowledge about crossing rivers or building bridges. When he did fall asleep in the wee hours of the morning, he had a nightmare, a nightmare of Sarah being led to the altar with another man. Awaking just before dawn, he went to the edge of the river to ponder. But as he paced near to where the bridge had once stood, a bird flew out of the bushes, hopping here and there looking for food. Suddenly, watching the bird, Samuel's heart leapt into the air with shock and wonder.

†

Meanwhile, the stern man who had lead Sarah away the previous day was none other than the Judge (he was also, as we met earlier, the sorcerer). His son had proposed marriage to Sarah, but when she turned him down in preference for Samuel, the Judge had been humiliated and her own family mortified. At the riverbank in view of Samuel that morning, the Judge had told Sarah to forget her worthless ideas about changing sides of the river and instead marry his very worthy son which would most certainly elevate and honor her family. If she didn't, the Judge promised, her parents would always suffer in the shame of her poor judgment. All day long the Judge and her parents implored her to think of others instead of just herself. They took turns casting doubt on the affections of Samuel, pointing out that if he really loved her, he surely would have found a way to get across the river by now.

Just before dawn, she yielded to their relentless pressure and agreed to marry the Judge's son, whom she had never been able to abide. Upon her acquiescence, the conspirators left quickly to make wedding preparations for that very day. Sarah fell into an uneasy sleep.

She dreamed a string of sorrowful dreams of forever being separated from Samuel. But then, in one dream, he came and tapped on her window and motioned for her to follow. She took only her shawl and followed him to the river's edge. The water churned and swirled and she wondered if this dream would end with both of them jumping into the deadly current. But in the dream Samuel picked her up and they seemed to climb into the air.

†

It was just as Sarah was acquiescing that Samuel had made his way to the river and was watching the bird. The little bird, hopping to and fro in search of a worm, had hopped — to Samuel's utter amazement — into thin air! Yet it seemed to be hopping on something solid, for its wings were still tucked. All at once, Samuel realized that the bridge was there, just invisible. Without a moment's delay, he set foot upon the place where the bird had hopped and found that his foot struck hard unseen stone. By placing one foot after the other, he made his way up to the highest point of the bridge, and there, gladness and trepidation competed for his heart — gladness because he was halfway across, and trepidation because nothing visible separated him from the raging waters below.

Reaching the opposite side and marking the bridge with a stone, he quietly sped to Sarah's house while the town still slept (her parents and the Judge being otherwise occupied and unsuspecting). Samuel was so relieved to find her there, alone. Motivated by the horror of his nightmare where she was marrying another, he took her away while she was still in the stupor of sleep and even had to carry her across the bridge.

When Sarah's town awoke and found her gone from her bed, there were many speculations about what had happened. Some said her disappearance confirmed that she was wicked and had caused the bridge to vanish. But one person claimed to have seen someone who looked like Sarah on the other side of the river walking with the young man named Samuel, but when the Judge heard about that, he had that person locked away for being a liar and a rumormonger (both considered serious crimes in that town).

The bridge never reappeared. Every now and again, however, a young girl from Sarah's side would disappear in the night and reappear on Samuel's side. And that is how it happened that the town on Sarah's side eventually died away, and the town on Samuel's side prospered and increased.

♪

Sassy Judy

Love is irresistible.

On a hill above the sea Sassy Judy taunted me. Peeking over daffodils she smiled and hummed and watched until, giving in, I met her eye — sprightly wink was her goodbye. Walking home I couldn't help being stunned by what I felt. Underneath my flaxen shirt, was my heart about to burst? Sassy Judy taunted me on a hill above the sea.

Somehow, she had dashed ahead and, pausing by my flowerbed, plucked the only rose I'd sown — seeing me she skipped on home.

To the village, to her street, seeking courage her to meet, I resolved that I would say, "For my red rose you must pay!" I rehearsed this in my mind, hoping Judy soon to find; turned the corner ... Standing there with the sunlight in her hair, holding rosebud offering, she tied my tongue without a string! Sassy Judy had caught me in our village by the sea.

Fumbling with my well-planned words, knowing now they seemed absurd, telling her that she should pay for the rose she stole today ... Oh, my heart and head did stir, what came out was one big blur. "Judy," I said breathlessly, "I think you should pay a fee for the ..."

Here I should have caught my breath, instead, embarrassed to death, I said,

"Judy you should pay a fee for the ...

… heart you stole from me."

Blushing red like rose she held, like a mighty redwood felled, like a contest when it's done, I was glad that she had won — plucking words right out of me like my rose beside the sea.

On that hill above the sea my sweet Judy walks with me. Hand-in-hand we stroll along joining in the seaside song:

> Come, come, sail away,
> For true love you'll never pay!
> Open sails, catch the wind,
> Love's a journey — Let's begin!

༄

The Lady

Evil is fueled by resentment. Love bears all things.

The deer looked on as the lady drove wooden stakes into the ground, marking the four corners of a future field. This was their land and they had roamed freely on it for uncounted years. The lady also belonged to this land but she had been away. Now she was much changed. In place of thick brown hair was something gray tied in a knot. Browned lined parchment covered where her fresh pink cheeks had been. Her deer-like slenderness was yet visible, but it was grown hard and sinewy. Only her eyes were unchanged, and this is how the deer recognized her.

When she had last rambled over these acres trying to coax the deer to eat from her hand, she had been a girl. On her return, she roved the land and watched the deer watch her, but she didn't sit like a statue with an outstretched hand as she had before. There seemed to be another purpose to her roaming, as was conveyed by the directness of her steps. The deer stayed on the edge of the woods, poised to take cover in case she did more than walk in one direction while counting, pound in a stake, walk in another direction, pound in a stake, and so on.

The lady was aware of the skittishness of the deer and remembered how they had once been her sole concern. When she was a girl she had done what everyone said couldn't be done. She had fed the wild deer out of her own hand and had even become so trusted among them that one of the fawns had lain down at her feet. While she pounded the stakes, she dreamed of being able to sit among the deer once again but knew that so much had to be done before that time.

Her youth and her beauty had been left in Africa. And now she was back on her own ancestral land where she had begun as a child, where she was always disproving the ones who told her what couldn't be done. By returning from Africa, she had now disproved those of her home country who had so long ago foretold that she would never come back from Africa alive.

The farm that her husband owned in Africa had sold for a price large enough to support her the rest of her widowed days. Now she had to prove the ones wrong who told her it was a mistake to sell the farm in Africa and return to a ruined house and a damp climate. They told her she would live out her days in loneliness and boredom, and they told her how awful the state of things was in the home country. They said she would be back. They said a wilderness back home is no substitute for being an owner of a large and lucrative farm in Africa.

The last stake was pounded in. It would take work to clear the plots to make them suitable for planting. It would take tools suited to the task, and it would take laborers to work the tools. All this the lady planned out as she marked the corners of each field. The region around her inherited land was full of unemployed men who had been displaced by machines and modernization. There were plenty with the skills to work a farm who needed work and success.

It was customary for the lady to seek no counsel except her own conscience. She knew too well that counsel usually dampened her best ideas and cautioned her to scale down her plans. Without appealing to anyone for advice, she had managed the renovation of the ancient home, installing heat and water, and eliminating drafts. Construction was also begun on a large outbuilding some distance from the house. Its twenty rooms, kitchen, and common room were comfortably furnished beyond what farm hands would expect.

With the dormitory now ready, the lady advertised for farm hands. She was straightforward about the type of work that was needed as well as the accommodations, and that the first twenty who showed up had the best chance of being hired.

Early in the morning of the day specified in the advertisement for interviews, the lady noticed five deer meandering close to the house. As she prepared the list of questions for the interviews, the deer might have gone completely unnoticed except that one hungry doe nibbled off some leaves of a bush which stood outside the window of the den. As soon as the lady saw them, the five started off toward the woods.

Applicants soon gathered on the lawn, and in each interview the laborers were asked about previous work they had done and the interest they had in farming. One who had worked his own farm before and was somewhat older than the rest was selected as foreman. None had been turned away as two less than twenty had come on that day.

The lady stood upon the steps of the house as the newly hired farm hands stood in the lawn with the foreman positioned halfway up the steps, per her instructions. As a group, she welcomed them to her land that was, as could be seen, uncultivated but ready to be broken. She promised them fair working conditions and payment at the end of each week, and then she introduced them to their new foreman. It was the foreman who would oversee the progress of the work, though she herself also would regularly visit the fields.

Among the newly hired workers were many desperate for income. That the job included a salary and room and board was beyond any employment they could have found elsewhere. Besides that, they were desperate for the feel of work. Many had sat idle and despairing, and just to wield a tool and develop an appetite again would be worth working for.

However, there was one who was not so desperate for work. He was not bound to that geographical area by family and ancestors as the others were. He could have gone numerous places in the world to work but happened to be in the vicinity of the lady's farm at that time and saw her notice for workers. Recognizing her name, he wanted to be hired just to see how far he could advance. It was a relief that he hadn't been chosen for foreman. His methods worked out best when he was one among the underlings.

The wilderness gradually transformed into a modest farm. With the fields cleared, the ground was tilled and planting was done. At each step the lady took an avid interest in the progress and the working conditions of each farm hand. She walked informally through the fields while the work was being done and asked one after another if they were satisfied with their work and their lodging and whether or not their salary was adequate. Many found that as a result of her inquiry, they were given a more suitable task or a slight raise in pay.

For some months, nothing untoward happened in the life of the lady or the workings of the farm. The lady took satisfaction in the successful operation of her plan. Even the foreman turned out to be a manager of her liking and she was glad to not have to replace him. None of the other farm hands required dismissal either. All the while, the deer fared well but kept their distance from both house and field.

One day as the lady was walking back from the woods where she had been seeing to a salt lick for the deer, one of the field hands hailed her. She had often noticed how mannerly he was in conversation, and how educated, though not quite as robust as the others. And it had struck her that farm work was unusual for such a one, but she didn't like to assume that people must only live within certain boundaries. The lady believed that a young man might take to farming for reasons other than laboring and earning a living, and therefore she never intruded.

The young man, whose name was Edward, doffed his hat and bid the lady a pleasant day, as was his custom. But then he uncharacteristically asked a question. He asked if she missed Africa. This startled the lady a bit that one of the hands should ask her such a question, but she overrode her surprise and answered affirmatively. The young Edward wasn't finished, however, and he persisted in saying that he missed it as well. This further surprised the lady, and it was her turn to ask questions of Edward, which is exactly as he had planned it.

In the course of a short conversation, Edward let it be revealed that he was likewise connected with a farm there but stopped short of saying that his father had hated the lady's husband. He only drifted off into sentimental reminiscences of his boyhood on the continent and finished off by politely thanking the lady for hiring him to work on her farm, pledging to do whatever work was needed to be done, regardless of its humbleness.

To know that there was one on her farm with a common experience in Africa and with whom she could converse about the life there buoyed the lady's spirit; yet, at the same time, she puzzled to place the young man, Edward, among the people she had known. When she returned to her den to light her evening fire, the doe was again nibbling the bush, causing it to tap against the window. By the time the lady made her way out with a carrot in her hand, the doe was gone.

In the dormitory Edward found himself the object of interest. The others had noticed his conversation with the lady, although it hadn't been long. The look and sound of it had been different than their own conversations when she had asked after their conditions. Edward was peppered with questions as to the nature of the exchange. He had never told any of these farm hand comrades about his own background, so it was with relish that he revealed it to them now, adding a broad hint that the lady had left Africa under suspicious circumstances and was not as well off as she pretended to be. However, Edward attested that he would stay working on the farm even if it didn't make a profit, and even if salaries did get lowered.

No thought like this had ever been brought up before in the dormitory. Some of the farm hands were reluctant to believe there could be any chance of the farm not making a profit or of the lady lowering a salary, especially since she had already raised theirs upon hearing of the number of people they had to support. Their protests in favor of the lady were easily outweighed by Edward's exclusive knowledge of Africa.

Some of the farm hands were intrigued by concealed information or any suggestion of mystery. In them, Edward had an attentive audience. He led them on far into the night with stories of which only he knew and begged them to keep silent about what they had heard since the lady's reputation was at stake. They promised, but only if Edward would continue to include them in his confidences.

The next day as the lady neared the fields, she was still trying to place Edward among the many she had known in Africa. She had intended to ask him his family name, but he spoke to her first, gushing politeness and subservience, and pleaded with her to allow him to do the most menial of farm labor, and to speak to the foreman about it on his behalf. Edward philosophically praised the virtue of building character through lowly work.

So he was assigned to the shoveling of manure onto the planted fields. He joined others who carried out this most unpleasant task. When the others asked why he had been assigned to it, he cast his eyes sideways and shrugged his shoulders, saying it had been the lady's decision. Then he let it slip that he knew too much about her; and besides, her husband had treated his father this same way.

The lady was unaware that morale was slipping and sliding downward, and that her attentions to Edward were giving him credibility among the farm hands to further cast doubt on her character and her intentions as their employer. She was aware that the foreman was having some difficulty where there had been none before, but in a manager's experience, she knew trouble could surface and be quelled in a never-ending cycle.

Some time passed. The lady continued to stop and chat with Edward, but he always sidestepped the topic of Africa. Yet Edward continued to feed the farm hands morsels of scandals, and the foreman did his best to keep the workers working. Then one morning, soon before the crop was to be harvested, the lady found the whole of her farm crew standing on the lawn before her front steps. They were agitated and quarreled with the foreman who had followed them there, but who had no part in their gathering. As the lady came out in response to the commotion, one of the boldest ones spoke. She listened to his accusations. She was accused of paying them less than other farms paid which had been carved out of wilderness, as well as planning to fire them all just after the harvest, replacing them with others who would work for a lower salary.

She looked around and didn't see Edward in the excited group of men, and she privately thought, it figured that he wouldn't be part of such a senseless challenge to her authority. When she had answered their charges and promised them continued employment based, of course, on their own willingness to work, she asked where Edward was. It was answered that he had gone into the woods to feed the deer, and again the lady thought, one could tell such a difference in people who had had a common experience in a foreign country.

After a conversation with the foreman, the lady decided to give all the workers a day of holiday just before the harvesting was begun. The news was greeted in the dormitory with wonder that a reward would be offered after they had so foolishly tried to mutiny. Sheepishly, they each left the farm, wondering how they could have allowed such fears to rise to such heights. Edward also left for his one day abroad in the region, but stopped by first to ask the lady if there was anything she needed from the merchants. He offered to use his day off to take her wagon to town to load up on any supplies she needed.

The lady was just about to consider the idea when the doe that had nibbled the bush by the den window limped into the yard. The doe, stopping on the edge of the lawn, gave a most menacing look at Edward. Edward doffed his hat in taking his leave, muttering that deer seemed to be unpredictable and he only admired them from afar and he would be going now and maybe he could drive the wagon for the lady later if she still needed the supplies. Then from the edge of the lawn he called back that he'd be happy to give up his day off for her if that's what she was asking. Of course, she politely declined.

Left alone on her farm, the lady looked at the doe and waited like a statue for the doe to approach, which it did, limping painfully across the turf. When the lady examined the leg, she found an unusual gash. As she tended the wound, the rush of words from Edward came back to her mind — the way he had turned it to make it seem like she had asked him to go gather supplies on his day off rather than it having been he who made the unsolicited offer. But especially, she remembered the strange way that the doe had looked at him which seemed to cause him to retreat. She puzzled this in her mind.

While the lady cared for the doe on her lawn, a fawn and three other deer in various stages of maturity approached. In the repose of the day, the lady sat still again among the deer that had once been her sole concern. She turned over and over the events that had preceded this day, the sudden turning of the farm hands, the absence of Edward, the trouble the foreman had had, and she resolved to find out the source of the trouble.

When the farm hands returned they set about to harvesting. The day was long and the men were too tired to listen in the evening to Edward's revelations, not to mention still feeling the sting of having staged a challenge on the lady's lawn which he stayed away from. He took it as a rebuff and stormed out of the dormitory in protest.

The lady customarily took early-morning and after-dusk walks among the deer. She had found her former seat from where, as a girl, she had lured the deer to approach. It was while she was sitting as silent and watchful as a deer that Edward came blustering into the area with his pockets bulging with rocks. It only took one rock thrown from his vicious hand at a deer to make the lady stand and reveal her presence.

Edward was clearly stunned, but mastered himself. From his depths came out all the injustices he had suffered at the hand of the lady and her kind. He saw that he was finished in the service of the farm, so he held nothing back. The lady was cursed for her lineage, her land, her inherited wealth, as well as her success in Africa. Edward spewed like a rancid geyser. With each invective he tossed down a rock until his feet were ringed with the tools of his cruelty. The lady said nothing. She merely stood her ground, resolutely knowing that she would have to respond to him as a wild animal if he made any move to attack.

But Edward was a coward all the way through. His next to last act was to announce in the dormitory that he had been fired for going into the woods and being too close to the lady's precious deer. Some of the farm hands who were weary of harvesting and fancied a return to idleness followed Edward. They thought they were making a brave stand to leave a job that fired a worker for looking at the deer, but they hadn't intended to do what Edward did. When he struck the match, they were dumbfounded. And when one field after another became consumed in flame, they ran off down the road, feeling foolish again for following Edward's lead.

The lady assessed the damage the next day and sadly announced that the farm was inoperable and, therefore, she was unable to keep on any farm hands. Each who had stayed innocently behind was sent off with a generous severance pay.

In time, weeds and brush grew up where the plots had been cleared. As the wilderness returned, the lady's mind turned and turned with the voices of old telling her again what couldn't be done. Then she made preparations. She had everything she needed. She allowed the wilderness to become what it was naturally, a deer park; and she opened the dormitory to small groups of sickly children and youth, inviting them to freely roam the land and find solace in the form and eyes of the deer. Some came for just a day, others stayed for prolonged periods of time. She frequently roamed the land with her young guests and entertained them with stories of Africa and days gone by. Always, the deer would come near and some would even snatch corn from timid offering hands, but only the lady ever had fawns lay down at her feet.

♪

LEATHER ROSE

(A rap response to W.M. Blake)
Evil peddles false beauty. Love is beauty.

O Rose, thou art frail: at the height of thy bloom thine Enemy seeks to hasten thy doom. So, constantly guard thy crimson delight and hold tight thy petals with all of thy might. The Enemy sniffs thy scent in the air; he salivates for a meal so fair.

But coming down path all dressed in green is striding a gardener, confidently. Pausing by another rose across from thee, he touches her petals and says he perceives that something so fragile, something so free, has no real defense from the Enemy. Something he holds in his gardener's sack he says will repel most any attack. He only asks one thing of red rose — to let him now of thorns dispose, saying that thorns are no real defense against worms seeking a crimson tent.

With thorns removed, he begins the task of making each petal eternally last. From his sack he pulls a vile of tannin, a natural substance like vitamins; it's used on horses — it takes their skin and turns it to rawhide (which is no sin). With tannin he paints each petal of the rose and turns them to leather so that each petal grows stronger and tougher, thick and wide, ensuring that no worm can enter inside.

O Rose, thou dost see thy neighbor's demise: exchanging her weakness for tanner's dark dye! And now the gardener has thee in his view. He touches thy petal! What wilst thou do?

"You weed!" The gardener curses and cries! His blood's on thy thorn, he spits in thine eye! Then cursing again he calls for the worm that flies in the night through the howling storm to enter thy chamber and riddle thee through, gnawing and chomping, exacting his due. Invisible worm with daggered eyes, how thinly veiled is your disguise! O Rose, to fend off one enemy invites the Foe of viler degree.

Thy neighbor of leather, unmoved by pain, smirkingly asks, "What is there to gain in jabbing the gardener, causing him pain? How can your temper be so untamed?! Reply!"

†

"Reply?! If roses are red, then what is your hue as you've been tanning out in plain view? You call yourself *rose with a leathery scent*, but what's in a name? O Shakespeare, lament! As for me, I stand with thorns in my side; the fact I'm a rose I dare not hide. If God meant a rose to be leathery and live saddled in security, I'd fain lose all thorns and leather become, but I'd be a whip and I'd crack till I'm numb.

"A rose I am, and a rose I'll be, embroiled in the ageless mystery of beauty midst war which can't be won — the worm finds a nest when each day is done. Yet …

"In standing, I've won."

♪

Cause for Alarm

Evil restricts possibilities. Love increases them.

Her grandmother's grandmother worked on a farm, while her grandmother's mother became a schoolmarm. Her grandmother was a first woman in space with whom her own mother continually raced. The daughter, herself, was the cause for alarm when she just decided to work on a farm.

ೆೋ

THE ARCHITECT AND THE ARTIST

Evil is a thicket. Love cuts through.

Take a walk with me and let me tell you a story.
Is it a new story?
It's a new story.
Does it have a happy ending?
Maybe.
Are you going to make it up or is it true?
You tell me after I tell it.
Okay, I'm ready.
Let's take this path through the meadow and I'll begin the story. Do you see that cottage over there with the red tiled roof? Let's go look into the windows and see what we see. That house is the first part of my story. Just peek in carefully now so that they don't see you. Tell me what you see.
I see a father and six children.
Do they look unhappy and weary of their lives?
Their house is very small and they are all together in the sitting room, but no, they look most happy and content to be together. The children are playing a game and laughing as one of them holds up a small piece of paper. I wish I could hear what they are saying. The father is writing, no, drawing, at a desk, and smoke is curling up around his head from his pipe. Every now

and then he looks up and motions everyone to come see what he is drawing. Everyone comes and looks and then all the children clap their hands and bound around the room.

Look around carefully. Is there not a mother in the room, perhaps lying as an invalid on a bed in the corner?

No. Wait, I see her now. She's carrying something out from the kitchen on a tray. Everyone gathers around to smell it. Oh, I wish I could smell it. But first, the father is showing her what he drew at his desk. She also claps her hands and does a spin around the room. What makes them so happy? Was the mother supposed to be an invalid? And what is it that the father draws?

I can't tell you that part of the story yet, but I can tell you that you have seen a happy ending, or, I should say, a happy middle, for those children are still not grown up and that family has many more years to live. But there is another part of this story.

Is it also as happy looking?

Perhaps if we see it only at a distance it will look happy, but we must go and peek into the windows to see it for certain.

Will I get to find out what game the children were playing and what it was the father was drawing?

For the present, let's continue our walk and unravel the story. We'll have to begin more at the beginning now that you have seen the end, or the middle. See that house way up there upon the hill? That's where we are headed.

Are you sure it's part of the same story?

I'm sure. Let me start at the beginning. There were once two sisters.

Don't forget to say ' Once upon a time.'

All right. Once upon a time there were two sisters. They shared a room as they were growing up, as well as had identical toys. One was a little older than the other but not so much that they couldn't play together.

Did they look alike as some sisters do?

No, one was dark and the other was light. One always smiled and was helpful and happy, and the other always frowned and complained and demanded to be served.

Oh, I know this part. And a wicked stepmother came and preferred one to the other. Then a handsome prince came and swooped one of them off her feet.

Not quite, but ... look out!

What was that?

That was the carriage belonging to the house at the top of the hill. I'm glad I pulled you away in time. It was going at full tilt apparently not caring who was on the path.

Look at it go! It's really kicking up the dust. Who was in it?

The other sister. She's always in a hurry. Before I finish the beginning, let's have a look in her house. Now, at this house you must be very careful about peeking into the windows and you'll probably have to peek in a lot of them before you can tell me what you see.

In this window I can't see anyone, but it looks like a very nice house. There is a piano and there are shiny tables and soft couches, but no one is here. Over in this window I see one child sitting by herself at a table eating. The food looks good but she doesn't look happy. Do you think she was made to eat alone? Wait! She's getting up and running into that room over there. I have to find that window. Oh, now here it is. Wow! It's a huge room with shelves and shelves of toys, and there's a boy running around in the center of it holding a doll above his head. The girl reaches for it, and, oh, the boy hits the girl. And here comes the mother. The one from the carriage, I guess. Her hands are raised and she is shouting. The boy shouts back at the mother and the girl shouts at him and the mother shouts at her and then they all shout at once. Let me look into another window. I've seen enough of that one. Here's a quiet scene. It must be the father. He's also drawing something at a desk, but it's a large high slanted desk. His head is bent low and he is going back and forth over a paper with some kind of measuring tool. Oh … what's this? The mother appears at the door. She doesn't look happy to see what he is drawing like the other mother was. She is talking and gesturing, and now the father stands up and goes towards her, and … he shuts the door! My goodness, what did he do that for? Now he is sitting down again and working with his tool, drawing lines on his paper.

Have you looked into all the windows?

I think so, except maybe one. Here is one. Oh, there aren't any people here, just carriages. One, two, three. With just one more there would be one for each person. I've peeked into the windows. Now where's the story? I can't figure it out.

OK, I'll back up a bit. Now both sisters got married in the same year. Of course, the older one had always considered herself more worthy than the younger one of marriage and romance. She had always looked for and expected the affections of young men, and when she received such, she shunned the presence of the younger sister, disdaining her very words and actions. In fact, the older sister hissed at the younger to disappear, or at least to freeze in her footsteps so as not to embarrass the older by her clumsiness and bad looks. 'You don't want to be a silly distraction to my young man and make him forget that he was about to lavish affection upon me, do you?'

Did the younger sister actually go along with this charade?

She did, unfortunately, but at the same time she felt she truly loved and adored her older sister and therefore didn't mind doing what she could to help romance bloom for her older sister. The younger sister knew too well how much and how often the older sister dreamed of being found by a prince and of being carried off to a castle where she could live in splendor and comfort and merit the respect of all the others. You see, whenever they had played with their porcelain dolls, which were identical, the older sister had always assumed the role of the girl waiting for her prince and her doll had always been the one dressed in gowns and jewels and lying upon a bed draped in sheer curtains.

What part did the younger sister's doll play? Couldn't hers have been another would-be princess waiting for another prince?

Perhaps between two other sisters it could have been so, but between these two sisters, only one was allowed to be the future princess and the other had to be her maid. This was the only story the older sister would agree to when they had played together, otherwise, she wouldn't play and the younger sister truly thought she enjoyed playing dolls with her older sister, and so she consented. Besides, it didn't matter to her that she was the maid because she knew it was only a game. She was a very attentive maid and even was the one to usher the prince into the chamber to find the waiting princess doll.

If I had been her, I would've said that my doll had to play the princess part at least half the time. Why was she willing to be the maid and not try to get the prince for herself?

Clothes.

Clothes? What do you mean?

The older sister's doll had the proper princess clothes and the younger sisters' doll had only the simple cotton dress that she came with from the doll maker. The older sister had pointed this out to her when the younger had suggested that she be the princess for once. The older sister's doll had a box full of gowns and shoes and jewels which she had come by and she refused to share them with the younger sister's doll, and so convinced her that it was clothes that decided the roles.

This is unbelievable. Couldn't the mother make the older sister share? They did have a mother, didn't they?

They did have a mother and, by the way, we've come on our walk to another house. It's right here along this path.

I can't see it clearly. There are too many carriages in front of it.

Let's slip around the back and see if we can peek into the windows from there.

It looks like someone is about to get married.

And so they are. Tell me what you see.

I see a dark-haired girl wearing a beautiful full-skirted wedding gown turning around and around in front of a mirror, and a light-haired girl standing behind in a very simple wedding dress. The one in the wedding gown has stopped looking at herself and she's looking at the one in the simple dress. She makes her turn around and around and then—I can hear them—she says, 'Remember how we always promised to be each other's maid of honor. Isn't this a convenient way to work it out? Here put these flowers in your hair so you don't look so plain. Besides, we're saving Mother a lot of money.' Now I see a mother coming into the room. She looks like she's going to either burst with a smile or cry. I can also hear her speaking. She says, 'Oh, my oldest daughter is getting married. What a special day this is. The first wedding in the family.' Then she turns to the one in the simple dress and says, 'You'll be glad that you agreed to let your older sister have a double wedding with you and say the first *I do*, even though yours was planned for so long. It's just like you to be understanding and flexible. You're still having *your* wedding and helping out your sister since she had such short notice. I know I don't need to remind you how unhealthy it is for a family if the younger daughter marries first. Sometimes the older sister becomes an old maid and never leaves home. Too bad you couldn't be wearing a more ornate gown like your sister, but that's the one you chose, after all.'

Well, I can't believe what I'm seeing and hearing. I hope this is a made-up story, because if it isn't, I'd like to get in there and set them straight.

I'm afraid you can't do that. If you stepped into the story, it would all disappear and you would never get to find out what game those children were playing and what that father was drawing.

I'd like to at least go up to that girl in the simple dress and tell her there's a happy ending, or a happy middle.

Why? Do you think she expects there to be a sad ending to this story?

Well, she looks content enough but I can't figure out why she doesn't put her foot down and quit letting those two push her around.

At the moment, it would destroy her because, you see, she really does think that she is serving the older one of her own free will and in so doing, preserving what friendship they have.

Did I hear the mother say that she had been planning to get married for a long time?

She had.

Why did she wait? Why didn't she jump at the chance to play the princess role in real life, scoff at the idea that clothes decide who the princess is, and leave the older sister on the shelf?

To her this was no competition, and she wasn't intending to put anyone on the shelf. Besides, the younger sister and her bridegroom had to wait for him to finish his education before they could marry. It wasn't an easy time for her. The older sister and the mother often tried to change her mind.

Tell me what they did. I'm sure it was crafty.

First, they gave her a poisoned apple to eat and then they put magic combs in her hair …

They did not! You're telling tricks from other stories.

You're right. The tricks the mother and the sister used were not the kind that could be coughed up or pulled out of the hair. Their tricks were much more sinister because they had started their tricks a long time ago. From the time when the younger sister was very young, the mother had only praised her when she was happy and helpful and giving and forgiving. If she was any other way the mother turned a coldness towards her that made all the light go out of her life. However, when she became happy and helpful and giving and forgiving again, all darkness vanished and the home was a safe and cozy place once more. Now the mother wasn't this way with the older sister. She allowed her to be cold and calculating and demanding and begrudging, and the lights would also go out in the home if the older sister were challenged in this regard. The only way for peace and light to live in the home was to please the older sister and therefore please the mother and, since the younger sister preferred peace and light to darkness and strife, she fell into their trick at a very early age.

I wish I had been there to tell her what was happening. That is a very crafty trick, but what good did it do them?

It served them, because they liked to be very busy, and the younger sister was always there to assist them. To top it all off, she assisted full of smiles, convinced that she was important in keeping the home full of light and peace. Her aim in life had been narrowed down to helping them with their lives and it seemed to her that theirs were very important lives to help. Now, what was I getting at? Oh, yes, how they tried to keep her from marrying her bridegroom. Can you guess?

Well, first the older sister would've acted unhappy about it in order to make the mother unhappy in order to disturb the peace in order to make the trick work. Thus the younger sister should've given up what made the peace fly away.

That's exactly what the mother and the older sister were depending upon. They had laid their trick so carefully for so long, and it had always worked before. You can imagine how sorely aggravated they were when it didn't work this time. The older sister was openly jealous and demanded to see the younger sister more often. The mother claimed to need the younger sister's help because her important life was suffering. They turned their coldest shoulders towards the younger sister, but she resisted giving up her plans to marry.

Oh, I'm glad to hear that the younger sister figured it out and didn't give in.

She didn't exactly figure it out. Though the younger sister was positive she had found her partner for life, she thought she could keep the two in balance by continuing to be the sister who was helpful and happy and giving and forgiving. The mother and the older sister wanted her to go on in that way because they needed her for their own lives and were afraid of her future husband in case he might not allow her to continue to serve them. In fact, he had no such designs. He only loved the younger sister as purely as can be imagined and when she was with him she felt a new part of herself peeping out. After she had been with him, the mother and the older sister detected this new part of her peeping out and then they accused, 'Aha, you must be careful of him. We are sure he only wants you to become his slave and to serve his interests. He thinks he's a very important fellow, we can tell, and whenever you are with him, you are like a flower that wilts. He makes you less than you are.' At these words the younger sister wavered and wondered. She valued very much peacefulness and light, but ever since she had found her lifetime partner, it seemed to her that peacefulness and light were more often restless shadows.

Oh, those two connivers. How do they have the boldness to lie? What's going to happen? Is the younger sister going to believe them?

I'm sad to tell you.

Oh, please make it happy, don't let those two win.

Do you think I'm making this up or telling you a true story?

I can't tell, but in case you're making it up, let me suggest that the younger sister should have herself a good think and shut the door on those wretches.

Maybe later, but for right now in the story, why don't we leave the wedding window and look into this window on the farther side of the house?

What's she doing in bed?

Who?

The younger sister. She's lying there as pale as vanilla pudding. I'm confused. Is the wedding still going on?

It won't happen for a year. We move around in time very easily in a story. Is anyone else in the room?

I see a much younger version of the man who was the father from the first cottage. He looks like he's saying good-bye to her. They look very sweet together and the younger sister looks as radiant as vanilla pudding can.

Is that it? Just the two of them looking like sweet desserts?

No, you won't believe this, but the mother is standing outside of the room. I can see the tip of her shoe sticking out across the doorway. Is she so desperate that she must eavesdrop?

Keep watching and keep me posted.

All right. Her toe isn't moving, but I can see that the future husband is leaving, perhaps for a long time. He's got a satchel of books and a suitcase.

Most likely he's going back to the University.

Now everything's moving fast. The shoe quickly disappears from the doorway. He leaves. The pudding has lost its shine. The closet door opens, and out slithers the older sister. This is a great story. How do you think all this up? Now, the older sister is at her bed and says, 'You look awful. I didn't mean to listen but it's clear that he wants to master you. You shouldn't be mastered by anyone. The next time he comes he'll have to deal with me first.' Before the younger sister can say anything, the mother comes sailing into the room with a fistful of letters. She's saying, 'I've never seen you looking so worn out. If he would stay away, I think you could get well.' And before the younger sister can reply her mother's reading bits from each letter. One person says, 'Tell her that her aunt hopes she gets well soon and learns to stand up for herself.' Another person says, 'Sickness doesn't run in our family so something must be terribly wrong.' The next letter says, 'Women in our family are strong and we know she won't be down long before breaking things off with him.'

Well, what does younger sister say to that? And what's the older sister doing?

The older sister is picking up the rose that the departing future husband left on the bedspread and she's trying to get it into a vase. No, what's she doing! She's, she's snapping the stem. The rose droops over like it's ashamed. I can see her, but she's hidden from the younger sister's view by the mother who is sitting upon the bed and opening letters. The younger sister only says, 'I think I could sleep.' But the mother wants to read her bits from more letters to *encourage* her. The younger sister listens meekly and smiles frequently. Then one letter promises to send her some flowers. That makes her look at the rose in the vase and then at her older sister, who looks mad and says, 'He's even too cheap to buy a proper rose.' Now as if by a pre-arranged signal, both of them leave. They seem to be connected in everything they do.

What do you think of the younger sister?

I'd like to get in there and tell her that I saw the older sister snap the rose and that I saw the mother's toe in the doorway, and I'd like to find out if she knew the older sister was in the closet. She doesn't seem to speak up for herself enough.

It might seem that way, but some people speak in other ways. Did she go to sleep?

No, she's writing a letter.

It's not good manners but just this once, you are allowed to read a letter that is not written to you. But don't ever try it outside of a story.

Wow, she writes in fast speed. It's addressed to her Intended. The first page is already full of wedding ideas—the date, colors, music, flowers, and food. The second page is recounting all the words of wisdom from her relatives. It seems she thinks they really care about her though she thinks most of them have never been in love. She has even written that the older sister was hiding in the closet, which must be not taken too seriously since the older sister is just protective and concerned about her since she is sick. Will the letter get sent or will those two censor it?

Oh, no. Letters are sacred and cannot be tampered with. That would be an obvious interference, and as you have seen, they are quite adept at covert practices.

The situation seems unbearable. Someone needs to help her see through them.

Someone does, but not directly. He draws her so tenderly to be his companion that she can never believe he wants her for a slave. All she can imagine is going through life with him. Eventually, she overcomes her sickness at just about the same time as she decides to turn a deaf ear to everyone's warnings.

So she *does* tell those two to take a hike!

Never. That would be entirely out of character, and the people in my stories are always in character. She merely is determined to get married, but she seems to be devoted to everyone at the same time. This is frustrating for the older sister and the mother because they are unsure whether she has discovered their methods or not. You see, they expected her to do what they would have done had they been treated as they treated her. And not until they put the question to her about sharing her wedding day did they know if they still had her in their trickery.

Oh, and they did. It's obvious from the wedding window where she was in the background and the older sister was being the beautiful princess. That was a real low spot.

You'd never have gotten the younger sister to agree with you on that. She was impossibly happy that day. Regardless of the conspiracy of others, that was the beginning of her life.

Is that when they moved into that little cottage in the meadow that we saw?

Oh, it's much too soon for that. That happened only after … well … let's walk into the town over there and look into a window of a building. There's something going on in there and if you look, I can tell you the next part of the story.

This is definitely not a house. It's a kind of office. Men are sitting at desks drawing on large pieces of paper. A few women seem to be helping the men by bringing them more papers. Oh

... I don't think I should tell you what I just saw. I'm sure it doesn't have anything to do with this story. But just the same, it did happen, and you did tell me to look into this window.

You'd better tell me because you never know.

Well, one of the men who is drawing, well, when the woman came to his desk to give him some papers ... uh ... he grabbed her hand before she could let go of the papers and kissed it, and then she pulled it away and looked angry, but the man just smiled at her and raised his eyebrows up and down.

Well, for certain it's not what I wanted you to look into the window to see, but nevertheless, you saw it. Perhaps it's part of another story that's being told. But look around the room and see if you see anyone you've seen before.

Oh, yes, I can see through an open door to a private office. There I see the younger sister and her husband. They have just laid a bag of money on the desk.

Who's behind the desk? Anyone familiar?

Yes, the father from the second house we saw, the older sister's husband, the one who was drawing at his high table while his children were fighting, who shut the door on his wife. But what is going on? Why are they giving him money?

They aren't actually giving him the money. They are asking him to build them a house. He's an Architect and he builds houses for people, but he usually builds grand houses with pillars and porticos and curved staircases and circular drives. They only want a cottage.

That's kind of nice, isn't it, for him to do that for them? Why is it that I feel that something not nice is going to happen? Is he going to really build it? Is he going to leave out something important when he builds it?

You ask a lot of questions.

I guess I'm just prepared for some kind of trick because obviously the younger sister is not serving the older sister and the mother, and it just looks like that man behind the desk is smiling too much at them. He wasn't smiling when he was in his house, and he *was* involved in stealing the wedding day. I suppose, it looks somehow unnatural that he's being so nice and attentive.

We can come away from the window now. You've seen the next part of the story, plus a little bit from another story, I must say. Now I'll tell you that the younger sister and her husband agreed to let the Architect build their house because he told them that he had a special way of making a fabulous house for a small amount of money. Of course, he said he was accustomed to building very large houses for very rich people, but as a favor to them as family of his wife, he would agree to build them a house, even though he said it would take him as much time and effort to build a small one as it did to build a very large one.

That can't be true, can it?

No, but what did the younger sister and her husband know about building houses? The truth was, the Architect was in a bit of a slump with no large houses to build, and the older sister was afraid of him failing and being without work, so she hatched the idea that he could build small houses as favors to poorer folk. It would make the Architect appear generous and keep the money coming in.

By the way, did anyone ever stop to think that a lot of small houses together might surpass the income of the larger ones?

No one really knew how many small houses there were, but it was only maintained that the older sister's husband was doing a great and generous service for less well-off folk. The younger sister and her husband had been happily living on the second floor of a rented house in town, but the younger sister saw a chance to serve the older sister by giving the Architect business, and she hoped there might be some reciprocation.

Is that some special feature on a house?

No, silly. That means since she did something thoughtful for the older sister, she hoped the older sister would do something thoughtful for her, such as begin to accept her husband instead of despise him.

I wish she could just see through the schemes and live her own life.

If she could, there would be no story to tell and this would be a very boring walk.

I hate boring walks.

I know, so back to the cottage and the small bag of money. The Architect promised to do his best with such a small sum.

Oh, I get the most awful feeling that something is going to happen with that small house.

There is something that happens with that small house but I don't think you can guess it. First, the Architect chose a beautiful piece of land to put the cottage on. The older sister whispered to the younger that this was a coveted spot by those who wanted to build big houses, but the Architect was giving it to them because he was so generous and wanted to see them living in a good spot for raising children. The hopes of the younger sister rose upon hearing this, and she concluded that her husband must not be despised anymore. She felt extremely happy and hopeful about the future and even confided in her older sister that her husband hoped to start a school in their town. So when the Architect told them that there was a delay because certain materials could only be ordered in large amounts and that he had to wait for more orders to build more small houses, neither the younger sister nor her husband knew to be suspicious. And even when he solemnly apologized that it was going to cost more than he expected, they completely trusted him, even when it caused them to go into debt. You see, he told them that he could still build them a house with their small bag of money but with the rising costs of building materials, it would only be a one-room bungalow. He would be glad to do it, but he foresaw a problem because that particular piece of land came with a legal requirement to build a house of a certain size. If a smaller house was put there someone could come along later and have it removed so they could build a bigger one. His advice was to take the long-term view of things and go into a little debt in order to avoid being chased off that land in the future.

Boy, I can't tell if they are stupid or the Architect is smart.

Well, sometimes, if people truly possess virtues and don't merely make a pretense of having them, someone who is cunning can use those virtues against them and make them look stupid.

I don't really like to hear the moral of the story. That usually means it's over. Did they get out of this mess?

Unfortunately, the younger sister and her husband had to live abroad for many years to make money to cover the debt that they owed on the small house.

Where did they go? What did they do?

They sold themselves into slavery as ship rowers and rowed around the world for seven years.

You're pulling my leg. They wouldn't do that.

Why not?

Because I have a hunch he's quite talented.

He is. What do you think he does?

Well, in their cottage he was drawing something—something that made everyone happy. I think he's an artist, isn't he?

Aha! You guessed it. In fact, he is a very talented artist and they all must go to Paris so he can teach because there is a much higher demand for art instructors there than anywhere else. Even though it is his dream to make art more available in his hometown and even open a school for the arts, he has no choice at this juncture.

Hey, aren't we in the same meadow where we started this walk? Where's the cottage? What's that huge building doing there?

Ahhh! That's the question that will start me on the next part of the story. That's a new cathedral. Let's pause here and look at it. You can't see it so well if you are up close. Isn't it beautiful? Doesn't its architecture match the surroundings?

Well, personally, I liked the cottage but I can agree that it is a magnificent building. How did it get here? Did a good fairy come and cause the small humble cottage to grow into a huge glorious church because the Artist had been so noble in his sufferings?

Your head is too full of fairy tales. No, there is a much more realistic explanation. Want to peek into some more windows? Woops, there are no windows. We'll have to settle for this door. Just remember to be silent, and don't try to enter the story no matter what you see.

OK. Hey, it's not finished inside. It's still being built.

That's right. Do you recognize anyone?

There's the Artist. He's opening a roll of paper and showing it to a man in a long robe. He's gesturing towards the ceiling and to the walls, and he looks very excited like he did in the cottage. But the man in the robe doesn't look happy. How can that be? He's positively frowning and shaking his head. Who is he?

That's the Bishop. He's the one who wanted to build this cathedral.

Oh, my gosh. There's got to be some mistake. He's violently shaking his head. He's rolling up the Artist's papers. He's bending them in half. He's throwing them on the floor. I've got to go in there. That's unbelievable after the Artist was so obviously enthusiastic.

Stand back and be quiet. Here comes someone.

Why, it's, it's the Architect. Maybe he's going to help.

Maybe, maybe not. Just watch.

All right. He—the Architect—walks up to the two of them. He has a funny look on his face. He doesn't even look surprised to see the papers on the floor. I think he's smirking, in fact. He looks like he's imploring the Bishop to reconsider ... no, no, no, not imploring. He's *apologizing.* He's apologizing to the Bishop for the plans of the Artist, but he's not looking at the Artist at all. He has turned his back towards him. He also is shaking his head over the plans and gives them a kick with his toe. The Artist, however, is watching the Architect very closely. His eyes are going back and forth between the Bishop and the Architect. Now he looks as if he just figured something out. Here he comes out the door. No, there he goes back in again. Ah, he had to go back for his drawings. Now, look out! Here he comes again. Let's follow him!

Wait a minute. Who's telling this story?

Well, you were doing a good job until now, but I think the story will tell itself if we just follow him.

If we follow him now we'll get ahead of ourselves.

Why, where's he going? Isn't he going back to his wife and children in the cottage?

He doesn't have a cottage. Don't you remember that his cottage used to be in this meadow?

Oh, that's right, and I had thought that his fairy godmother promoted him to a castle, before I looked in the door, that is. Now I'm confused. Okay, you can tell the story again.

Well, I'll try to tell it.

I hope you can hurry it up because I have to know if he's all right.

You've gotten a little more involved in this story than I had imagined. I just meant to entertain you for an afternoon's walk.

Well, in that case, you should've told me *Goldilocks and the Three Bears* or *Hansel and Gretel,* or some other made-up story.

But this is just a made-up story.

No, it's not.

So, you've decided, and we haven't even come to the end yet. What made you decide?

The way you acted at the cathedral door. I think you were surprised at what happened. I don't think you knew that part of the story. In fact, I'm sure I heard you gasp, and when you took my hand to walk away, you were quivering.

Can't a person quiver when they see something treacherous happen?

Of course, but they usually don't if they are making up a story to entertain someone for an afternoon's walk. So, please, proceed with this *true* story at your convenience.

Now you're a little too cavalier. This is the most difficult part of the story.

Perhaps you have a window for me to look into.

That's a good idea. But I'm afraid you'll have to look into it with your mind's eye. Remember the first window at the cottage? Well, that was just before the cottage was given up by the family so that this cathedral could be built.

Given up?

Yes. You see, they had come back from Paris to live in the cottage, and the father—the Artist—struggled to start a school for artists. He couldn't manage to enroll many students since art was considered a frivolous pastime. But fortunately, he owned the cottage since he had worked in Paris for so many years. He reasoned that if he could just take on a few students they could manage to survive. The whole town knew of his struggles, and while town folk praised the theory of being an artist, they actually thought he should have stayed on in Paris where artists seem to be thicker and obviously paid better, or that he should go into some other business. Some even suggested that since he seemed to like to paint, he could contract with the Architect to paint the houses he built, especially the big ones.

But why would he give up the one thing he owned?

For the cathedral. It will help to understand that the Architect was quite well known both for his architectural designs and his ability to build quickly and cheaply. The Bishop was on a budget and in a hurry. Therefore, it was not surprising that the Architect was approached by the Bishop to build the cathedral. The Bishop asked the Architect to not only design a modern cathedral but also to build it and have its interior painted. The Architect thought immediately of the Artist in the cottage, and why not? They had their wives in common. They lived only a stone's throw from each other. And the Architect knew the Artist was truly gifted. He told the Artist that the Bishop wants someone who can make the interior truly a place of beauty and splendor so that all who enter will be transported to heaven itself. The whole town admired the generosity of the Architect in giving the leg up to the Artist.

I have my suspicions.

Of course you do. That's because I'm a very good storyteller.

No, it's because I'm a very attentive listener.

All right. Now that we are both pleased with ourselves, let me continue. The Artist approached the task with reverence. He had only ever dreamed of such an opportunity. It seemed to him that now he could give full rein to his artistic vision and craft, and for such an admirable purpose, too. It was such an honor to be asked to transport people to heaven with your art. So, he began to make his drawings, consulting often with the Architect who told him what the Bishop wanted. At the many and various stages he climbed the hill to the Architect's house to lay out his designs. Though he had to suspend his teaching in order to make the detailed, intricate drawings that the Architect said the Bishop wanted, he knew that when the job was done he would be paid. And then he began to think that even if he weren't paid, he would still be willing to do the job.

I smell danger coming. He's too idealistic.

Perhaps. But wait until you hear this. One day, while the Artist was working on his drawings in the cottage and before any ground was broken for the cathedral, the Architect solemnly told him some hard news. He acted extremely reluctant to come out with it, leading the Artist to believe that the whole cathedral might be in jeopardy. The Artist was so distraught at just the thought that he vowed he would do anything he could to solve whatever problem there might be. And then the Architect came out with it. The Bishop had chosen the very land for the Cathedral that the Artist's house sat upon.

Now isn't that a coincidence?

Did I mention that the Bishop had also asked the Architect to select the best location?

No, you left that out.

So I did. Well, so did the Architect, in fact, when he told the Artist. But what do you think the Artist did when he heard?

I suppose I know. He gave up the cottage for the greater glory of building a cathedral that would transport people straight to heaven by its magnificence.

Don't make it sound so insignificant. That's exactly what he did, and he did it willingly and joyously, and no hardship mattered to him in this sacrifice. In fact the whole family was happy. You saw them through the window. They knew *then* that they were giving up the cottage. There was no sadness there. For them, their part in giving up their cottage was all part of a bigger picture where people make sacrifices for the good of others. In truth, they had no fear about their future. They only felt satisfaction that they had done what was right.

Oh, those poor dears. They must have been at the back of the line when skepticism was given out. You should have let me enter the story when I asked you. I could have saved them a lot of trouble.

Now listen to yourself. Would you really want to change them? Why do you think you are so interested in this story? Isn't it because there is something noble and innocent about these people?

Yes, but it's frustrating. I mean, to give up your house and to think you're doing it as a service to others. Even I know how others take advantage of such a sacrifice.

Maybe you do know, but remember you just want the story without any moralizing. It turns out that the Artist gave up his cottage and moved his family to a very small place in town. He watched the cathedral going up and was thrilled to see every new piece put in place.

Did the Artist have any ill feelings towards the Architect?

No. He spoke of the Architect in superlatives and never doubted that the design and the location were of one inspiration. Then, the day happened that you saw in the cathedral door. The Architect had set them up, as you might have guessed. Neither the Bishop nor the Artist had ever met since the Architect had been the sole communicator between them both. All discussions had gone through him. And the Artist certainly did not suspect the Architect of bringing him to ruin through the job he had given him. But clearly, the Bishop expected something far different than was shown him on that day in the unfinished cathedral, and the Artist was not even aware that he, through the Architect, had demanded higher pay from the Bishop. In fact, the Bishop reacted so violently against the Artist's plans and fired him so vehemently because of the many other things he had heard about him—things about his character and practices, especially in regard to money matters. Why have you stopped walking?

How can you tell me this in such a matter-of-fact way?

This is just the way it was.

But, this is betrayal at its most insidious. This is outrageous. You haven't done it justice. You should've spoken with more emotion. I mean, this makes the blood boil. The Architect entrapped the Artist, preyed upon his need to work, exploited his innocence and goodheartedness, tricked him out of his house, told lies about him, and then allowed the Bishop to make the fatal blow without stepping in to accept any of the blame. What kind of way is this for people to act, especially those charged with building a cathedral? I just think you have lost sight of the travesty of this story. I'm very disappointed with you as a storyteller, and I have to just sit here a moment and get over it.

Don't cry. It's going to be all right. I promise you.

Leave me alone. You can't tell me a story like this and then pretend that it's nothing. What's to become of the Artist and his children and his wife? Do you think they are not going to suffer and be forever humiliated? I remember how he looked when he walked away from the cathedral. There was something in him that was crushed. I'm afraid he will give up painting all together and the happiness of his home will be destroyed, and maybe even he'll die of despair. Some artists do die of despair, you know. And his children were so happy, but all that is impossible now.

Look; don't cry. Really, you got more involved than I thought you would. Perhaps I shouldn't have told you. Maybe you want to hear *Little Red Riding Hood*, and then we'll go home to tea.

You must tell me where he went when he left the cathedral. You said you would. And I want you to tell it with emotion. None of this cold-hearted narration. I'll stop you if you disappoint me.

You are a demanding audience. I'll try to give you what you want. The interview inside the cathedral had become known all over and it was accepted as fact that the Artist had tried to elevate himself both professionally and financially through the charity of the church. He was too stunned to give any kind of defense. You may not believe this, but since he had felt that he would be glad to do the job for nothing, if that were required, he came to believe he should do it for nothing, and because he enjoyed it so much, the remuneration really meant nothing to him. So when it became the crux of the gossip about him, he actually felt a true remorse that he had not done it without pay.

But he did nothing wrong. It was all because of the Architect and what he told the Bishop.

Yes, and after that day, the Artist was no longer welcome in the town. And he was penniless. And he was in debt. And he had a large growing family to take care of. And he had lost faith in all of humanity and gave up art. His whole world crashed and crumbled and turned inside out. Almost in a daze he sold everything he had and kept only those things he and his family needed immediately. With that amount of money he bought tickets on a ship that took them to the first of many places where he would work in a variety of jobs for long years to come. To say he lived an uncertain life is putting it mildly. During it all the whole family experienced everything together, all of them rising up in hopeful times and sinking low in times of despair. They suffered many deprivations, but what they suffered the most from was the betrayal.

What did the Architect and his family do all this time? Didn't they care? Wasn't there any sense of honor?

The Architect, his family, the younger sister's mother, the town, the Bishop, the cathedral—everything went on with no sign that anything inimical had happened.

Inimical?

Untoward. Indecorous. Unfavorable.

Oh, unfavorable. So, is this the end? I was led to believe that this story would have a happy ending.

Well, you know stories. One person's happy ending is another's demise. Just think of your nursery stories. It all depends on whom you're rooting for.

I suppose then that the Artist died in ignominy in a far-off land, but in some twisted way that was a happy ending because he gave what was necessary to build a beautiful cathedral in an idyllic location; and many people will remember him with awe and respect, that is, after some historian clears up the record about his alleged desire for more money. And the Architect lived a wonderfully prosperous life, which looked like a happy ending, but in reality, he never had another moment of peace after what he had done to the Artist.

So is that ending acceptable?

To a story connoisseur, such as I consider myself to be, it's only marginally satisfactory.

In that case, would you like to hear the actual end of the story?

Oh, I'm so glad there's more. I was a bit worried.

The Artist ended up in a faraway country, but not in the same happiness as he had lived in Paris. Now he felt like a foreigner, not just in that country, but in the world. They still had a happy home, but it was a poor home. One day something happened. He got a letter that had traveled all over the world to reach him. It had gone first to one place, then got forwarded to another, and so on and so on, traversing all the places he had previously lived, until the face of it was so covered with postmarks that where it had originated was a mystery to the Artist. One corner had gotten damp, smearing the sender's name as well. It was a thick piece of correspondence. The whole family gathered around to see this world traveler opened up. Besides, it had arrived at a most propitious moment.

Propitious?

Auspicious. Providential. Favorable.

Ah, favorable. Go on.

The letter told a most interesting tale of an earthquake, a fire, and a brick falling on the head of a Bishop. It also told of an investigation into the original construction of a certain cathedral by a certain Architect to find out what corners had been cut, making the whole structure crack. Since the Architect was indirectly involved in the death of the Bishop, a certain house on the hill was discovered empty one morning, the occupants and their fast carriages but a blur on the horizon.

So it was a victory letter?

Well, not exactly since the author had no sense of triumph. The earthquake had cracked, the fire had gutted, and the falling brick had left him in charge of the cathedral since he was a priest under the Bishop who had been felled, and thus the correction of all the aforementioned problems fell upon him. No, the letter was in large part an explanation, a pleading, and a request. The Priest had been but a seminarian when the Artist had been driven away from the town by the scandal of the cathedral business. He had remembered it always, but had had no forum to look into the matter until the death of the Bishop. His investigation had led him to the interesting discovery that the Bishop had in reality asked the Architect to build him a cathedral that was *absent* of any artwork. He had wanted the architecture itself to be the sole art, and for it to be so lofty and awe-inspiring that the peaks and sheer height replaced the need for any other expression. He wanted it to be modern. The Bishop's only need for the Artist had been to apply a coat of paint to the vast interior surfaces that were created by the Architect. The Architect, of course, was the only one who knew of the Bishop's real desire, and he built just what the Bishop wanted. As we know by the way the Bishop met his end, the structure was too ambitious and constructed too quickly. The writer of the letter had managed to repair the earthquake damage but had to lower the ceiling and remove the loftiness, resulting in an unadorned domed surface. He confessed that he was writing to the Artist because he had once caught a glimpse of the Artist at work and had seen something on his face that made him think the Artist could see into the next world and convey what he saw, using the earthly elements of which paint and brushes are made. So the Priest was asking the Artist to do the original work he had been commissioned to do.

Well, finally, something that sounds like justice.

However, the date on the letter was a matter for concern.

Oh, no, not another problem.

You remember how it had trailed his path. The Artist wondered if the Priest still needed him or if he hadn't possibly given up and commissioned someone else already. So the Artist put that letter in his pocket and considered what he should do. It would be a risk to return to the cathedral town if that were the case.

Is this where the propitiousness comes in?

Aha, so you remembered? By the way, am I telling this with enough emotion?

I won't complain.

It happened that just when the letter arrived, the Artist faced several dilemmas. He had been away a long time, his children were nearly grown and needed to be in their homeland, and the people of that land were becoming xenophobic.

Ooh! That sounds like a nasty disease. Was it contagious?

That's no disease. But it is contagious. It means the people of a place become fearful or hateful of anything or anyone that is foreign. When it happens it's better to be the most despised of the native people than to be a foreigner. Anyway, the Artist and his family faced a difficult time no matter which way they turned. Their options were few. Besides, it wasn't easy to travel in those days, a very circuitous route sometimes being the only choice, which made it dangerous as well. He had many heavy concerns. To start with, he could not sell what they had because no one would buy anything from a foreigner to avoid being accused of having sympathies towards foreigners. So he just left everything behind. It was even dangerous to give it away. He bought the best tickets he could, hoping to reach the cathedral town in time. It was a long trip, and it became longer and longer because of having to avoid certain dangerous locations in the world, not to mention that he had to work all along to pay for the next leg of the trip. The world seemed a most cruel place. It caused one to wonder if anyone in Heaven was watching or not.

I've begun to wonder that myself.

But the Priest had stubbornly waited upon the Artist, turning down many other artists with long lists of credentials who had arrived in the flesh ready to paint. He was reluctant to admit to anyone why he was not hiring any of them, and everyone became impatient with him. The town just wanted to put the whole matter behind them, and the unpainted interior was a most visible reminder of all that had gone on. Though the Priest had no assurances that the Artist had even received the letter, he promised the town that a master who was already familiar with the cathedral had been commissioned to do the work and was merely on his way, but he didn't dare tell them whom. Only long after the Artist had returned, and after those with long memories and suspicions had been quieted, and after the Artist had almost finished the work, did the Priest tell why he had been so sure and so stubborn on this point, and then he only spoke of it to the Artist. The Artist was cleaning his brushes at the end of the day and it was dark in the cathedral. Just a candle burned. The Priest wasn't sure how the Artist would accept the story he had to tell, so he approached the topic carefully. He knew there might be old wounds that would get opened up or regrets that were impossible to correct.

Could you please hurry up? I can't stand the suspense.

Well, so much for trying to go for effect. Next time I will tell you *The Three Little Pigs* and you will be one of them.

Sorry. It's just that I'm so impatient to find out, and I hope nothing else disastrous is going to happen.

The Priest told the Artist how he had been walking around the cathedral one day after the structural restoration had been completed, simply to reassure himself that the whole building was sound and that all scars from the earthquake had been healed. It was on this walk, while his gaze was drawn skyward, that his toe kicked against a piece of red roofing tile. It actually punctured his shoe, wounded his foot and drew blood, which so angered him that he searched the grass until he found what had cut him. Then he asked, 'Now what is this doing here? There are no such tiles on this cathedral. Who is using this ground as a place to discard broken materials?' When he sat down on the ground with that shard of tile in his hand, he didn't get up for a long time, and when he did, he was determined to send the Artist a letter and ask him to return. That half-buried piece of tile reminded him that the Artist had actually given up his own house—to which this red tile used to belong—so that the cathedral could be built—the building of which forced the Artist to leave—and that led the Priest to the conviction that the only artist who could restore the interior with any kind of vision and put the whole matter to rest was the one who had given up everything to do it and the one who had had everything taken away from him because of it.

What did the Artist say? Was he upset to hear about his cottage?

He was only silent. The candle burned and crackled. The Artist took his clean brushes and dipped them into the paint. He went back to work.

And the Priest? What did he do? He must have been confused.

No, I think the Priest understood the Artist's response. He left him there.

Some people just don't speak when you want them to. I would love to know what he thought.

Then, a most amazing thing happened. The Artist finished the fresco that night and just as he made the last stroke, there was another earthquake and the cathedral collapsed all around him and on top of him and he was buried under rubble.

Tell me you're kidding.

I am. It was the disaster you were dreading, wasn't it? Actually, the cathedral became a Mecca for artists of all sorts. In fact, the worshippers seemed to look up more than they did when the high ceiling was there. However, the Artist's health suffered tremendously. He had worked tirelessly in the drafty cathedral, very often working thirty-six hours straight if it meant finishing one scene. So by the time he was credited as the father of the re-renaissance of cathedral art, he was confined to his home and his pipe. Many people tried to see him to learn from him, but he saw few people and gave instruction to none.

In a sad way this sounds like the happy ending.

It is the end, and our walk is finished at the same time. What a coincidence.

Wait a minute. The walk is over and I never found out what game the children were playing in that cottage. You promised I would.

Oh, you're right. I did promise. To be quite honest, that was just some game we kids made up on the spot to occupy ourselves until the cookies came out of the oven.

Did you say 'we'?

Oui.

Afterword

From 'Frank' to 'Judy'

Evil shall end. Love never does.

What word, what art, what song conveys
The contents of a sigh?
My love, my spouse, for thee I pray
Strong sails to lift thee high.

This sigh suspires by joys we've gained
Through leagues of windward gale;
Your love it often did sustain
When tempest me impaled.

And once again our course has led
Into uncharted sea;
The sigh I breathed is gently said
In deep, deep love for thee.

www.ingramcontent.com/pod-product-compliance
Lightning Source LLC
Chambersburg PA
CBHW030852170426
43193CB00009BA/578